LifeChange

S E R I E S

A life-changing encounter
with God's Word from the book of

PSALMS

NAVPRESS

Discipleship Inside Out®

Discipleship Inside Out®

NavPress is the publishing ministry of The Navigators, an international Christian organization and leader in personal spiritual development. NavPress is committed to helping people grow spiritually and enjoy lives of meaning and hope through personal and group resources that are biblically rooted, culturally relevant, and highly practical.

For a free catalog go to www.NavPress.com or call 1.800.366.7788 in the United States or 1.800.839.4769 in Canada.

ISBN: 978-1-61521-119-7

Printed in the United States of America

6 7 8 9 10 11 / 19 18 17 16 15 14

CONTENTS

HOW TO USE THIS STUDY

Objectives

Most guides in the LIFECHANGE series of Bible studies cover one book of the Bible. Although the LIFECHANGE guides vary with the books they explore, they share some common goals.

1. To provide you with a firm foundation of understanding and a thirst to return to the book.

2. To teach you by example how to study a book of the Bible without structured guides.

3. To give you all the historical background, word definitions, and explanatory notes you need so that your only other reference is the Bible.

4. To help you grasp the message of the book as a whole.

5. To teach you how to let God's Word transform you into Christ's image.

Each lesson in this study is designed to take sixty to ninety minutes to complete on your own. The guide is based on the assumption that you are completing one lesson per week, but if time is limited, you can do half a lesson per week or whatever amount allows you to be thorough.

Flexibility

LIFECHANGE guides are flexible, allowing you to adjust the quantity and depth of your study to meet your individual needs. The guide offers many optional questions in addition to the regular numbered questions. The optional questions, which appear in the margins of the study pages, include the following:

Optional Application. Nearly all application questions are optional; we hope you will do as many as you can without overcommitting yourself.

For Thought and Discussion. Beginning Bible students should be able to handle these, but even advanced students need to think about them. These questions frequently deal with ethical issues and other biblical principles. They often offer cross-references to spark thought, but the references do not give obvious answers. They are good for group discussions.

For Further Study. These include: (a) cross-references that shed light on a topic the book discusses, and (b) questions that delve deeper into the passage. You can omit them to shorten a lesson without missing a major point of the passage.

If you are meeting in a group, decide together which optional questions to prepare for each lesson and how much of the lesson you will cover at the next meeting. Normally the group leader should make this decision, but you might let each member choose his or her own application questions.

As you grow in your walk with God, you will find the LIFECHANGE guide growing with you—a helpful reference on a topic, a continuing challenge for application, a source of questions for many levels of growth.

Overview and Details

The study begins with an overview of the Psalms. The key to interpretation is context (What is the whole passage or book *about?*), and the key to context is purpose (What is the author's *aim* for the whole work?). You will lay the foundation for your study of the Psalms by asking yourself, *Why did the author (and God) write the book? What was the goal? What is the book about?*

In lessons 1 through 10, you will analyze successive passages of the Psalms in detail. Thinking about how a paragraph fits into the overall goal of the book will help you to see its purpose. Its purpose will help you see its meaning.

Kinds of Questions

Bible study on your own—without a structured guide—follows a progression. First you observe: What does the passage *say?* Then you interpret: What does the passage *mean?* Lastly you apply: How does this truth *affect* my life?

Some of the "how" and "why" questions will take some creative thinking, even prayer, to answer. Some are opinion questions without clear-cut right answers; these will lend themselves to discussions and side studies.

Don't let your study become an exercise in knowledge alone. Treat the passages as God's Word, and stay in dialogue with Him as you study. Pray, "Lord, what do You want me to see here?" "Father, why is this true?" "Lord, how does this apply to my life?"

It is important that you write down your answers. The act of writing clarifies your thinking and helps you to remember.

Study Aids

A list of reference materials, including a few notes of explanation to help you make good use of them, begins on page 95. This guide is designed to include enough background to let you interpret with just your Bible and the guide. Still, if you want more information on a subject or want to study a book on your own, try the references listed.

Scripture Versions

Unless otherwise indicated, the Bible quotations in this guide are from the New International Version of the Bible. The King James Version (KJV) is also used.

Use any translation you like for study, preferably more than one. A paraphrase such as The Living Bible is not accurate enough for study, but it can be helpful for comparison or devotional reading.

Memorizing and Meditating

A psalmist wrote, "I have hidden your word in my heart that I might not sin against you" (Psalm 119:11). If you write down a verse or passage that challenges or encourages you and reflect on it often for a week or more, you will find it beginning to affect your motives and actions. We forget quickly what we read once; we remember what we ponder.

When you find a significant verse or passage, you might copy it onto a card to keep with you. Set aside five minutes during each day just to think about what the passage might mean in your life. Recite it to yourself, exploring its meaning; then return to your passage as often as you can during your day for a brief review. You will soon find it coming to mind spontaneously.

For Group Study

A group of four to ten people allows the richest discussions, but you can adapt this guide for other-sized groups. It will suit a wide range of group types, such as home Bible studies, growth groups, youth groups, and businessmen's studies. Both new and experienced Bible students will benefit from the guide.

The guide is intended to lead a group through one lesson per week. However, feel free to split lessons if you want to discuss them more thoroughly, or omit some questions in a lesson if discussion time is limited. You can always return to this guide for personal study later. You will be able to discuss only a few questions at length, so choose some for discussion and others for background. Make time at each discussion for members to ask about anything they didn't understand.

Each lesson in the guide ends with a section called "For the group." These sections give advice on how to focus a discussion, how you might apply the lesson in your group, how you might shorten a lesson, and so on. The group leader should read each "For the group" at least a week ahead so that he or she can tell the group how to prepare for the next lesson.

7

Each member should prepare for a meeting by writing answers for all of the background and discussion questions to be covered. If the group decides not to take an hour per week for private preparation, then expect to take at least two meetings per lesson to work through the questions. Application will be very difficult, however, without private thought and prayer.

Two reasons for studying in a group are accountability and support. When each member commits in front of the rest to seek growth in an area of life, you can pray with one another, listen jointly for God's guidance, help one another to resist temptation, assure each other that the other's growth matters to you, use the group to practice spiritual principles, and so on. Pray about one another's commitments and needs at most meetings. Spend the first few minutes of each meeting sharing any results from applications prompted by previous lessons. Then discuss new applications toward the end of the meeting. Follow such sharing with prayer for these and other needs.

If you write down each other's applications and prayer requests, you are more likely to remember to pray for them during the week, ask about them at the next meeting, and notice answered prayers. You might want to get a notebook for prayer requests and discussion notes.

Notes taken during discussion will help you to remember, follow up on ideas, stay on the subject, and clarify a total view of an issue. But don't let note-taking keep you from participating. Some groups choose one member at each meeting to take notes. Then someone copies the notes and distributes them at the next meeting. Rotating these tasks can help include people. Some groups have someone take notes on a large pad of paper or erasable marker board (pre-formed shower wallboard works well) so that everyone can see what has been recorded.

Page 98 lists some good sources of counsel for leading group studies.

INTRODUCTION

The Book of Psalms

The book of Psalms is a book of prayer, every conceivable type of prayer: prayers of worship and praise, confession and acknowledgment, intercession and supplication, protection and deliverance, vindication and forgiveness, renewal and restoration, reward and thanksgiving. There are prayer psalms offered up in times of spiritual darkness and challenge, when God appears to be silent or when all that is left to do is wait on Him. Many prayers in the Psalms look back on God's deliverance and give hope and confidence in God's sovereignty for everything that awaits us.

The prayers of the Psalms are prayers of deep emotion and feeling. The psalmists hold very little back in regard to their joy, sadness, fear, shame, and, in many cases, seemingly inconsolable rage. No matter. The God of heaven awaits on His throne, pleased to receive the prayers of His saints, especially prayers originating from the depths of their souls:

> The smoke of the incense, together with the prayers of God's people, went up before God from the angel's hand. (Revelation 8:4)

The purpose of this study is to broaden and deepen our understanding and experience of prayer by looking at the prayers of our spiritual ancestors in the Psalms: David, Moses, Asaph, and others. In the Lord's Prayer, Jesus showed us *how* to pray. The prayers of the psalmists give us a myriad of examples of what Jesus meant, examples God expects us to follow and emulate:

> Remember your leaders, who spoke the word of God to you. Consider the outcome of their way of life and imitate their faith. (Hebrews 13:7)

If there's anything we can learn about prayer from the Psalms, it's that God simply wants us to acknowledge what He already knows to be true—about our circumstances, our hopes, our desires—and, most of all, how we *feel* about all of those things.

9

Authorship of the Psalms

Seventy-three (less than half) of the psalms are attributed to David, with thirteen of those clearly identified with some period or event in David's life (3, 7, 18, 34, 51–52, 54, 56–57, 59–60, 63, and 142). Others include Jeduthan, the Sons of Korah, Asaph, Heman and Ethan the Ezrahites, Moses, and Solomon.

Many of the psalms are not attributed to specific authors but rather have general titles, such as "director of music" (which would indicate the psalm was to be used in temple worship). Or they are given musical or liturgical instructions, such as "for flutes," "according to sheminith," or "according to gittith" (indicating the type of instruments that should be used).

Literary Tools

Most of the psalms are poetic prayers that tap into a variety of literary "tools" in order to bring life and vibrancy to the psalmists' requests of God. Many of these devices are not obvious to us because they are tied to the original Hebrew in which the psalms were written. For example, some of the psalms are acrostics, in that each line starts with a different letter of the Hebrew alphabet (4, 25, 37, 111, 112, 119, 145). Other psalms make use of alliteration and assonance, in which certain sounds at the beginning or the middle of the words are repeated.

Other non-Hebrew-dependent literary devices include: *apostrophe*, in which certain aspects of nature are addressed as if they were persons (see Psalm 68:15-16); *hyperbole*, used to exaggerate a concept in the mind of the reader in order to call attention to its underlying core truth (see Psalm 40:12); and *inclusion*, a form of repetition in which the psalmist will begin and end a section of the psalm, or the entire psalm, with similar or contrasting statements in order to form verbal bookends for the prayer (see Psalm 70:1,5).[1]

Literary "genres" in the Psalms include prayers of praise, lament, worship, wisdom, and hymns.

What do we do with the psalms of cursing?

The "psalms of cursing" are known as the imprecatory psalms.
Here are excerpts from a few:

Destroy thou them, O God. (5:10, KJV)

May their path be dark and slippery. . . . May ruin overtake them by surprise. . . . May they fall into the pit, to their ruin. (35:6,8)

In your faithfulness destroy them. (54:5)

Let death seize upon them, and let them go down quick into hell. (55:15, KJV)

Consume them in wrath, consume them, that they may not be. (59:13, KJV)

Pour out thine indignation upon them, and let thy wrathful anger take hold of them. (69:24, KJV)

Add iniquity unto their iniquity: and let them not come into thy righteousness. (69:27, KJV)

Pour out thy wrath upon the heathen that have not known thee. (79:6, KJV)

Let the sinners be consumed out of the earth, and let the wicked be no more. (104:35, KJV)

The following psalms have some sort of imprecatory feature or appeal for vindication: 3, 5, 6, 7, 10, 11, 17, 23, 25, 28, 31, 35, 40, 41, 54, 56, 58, 59, 63, 68, 70, 71, 73, 74, 79, 83, 94, 97, 104, 109, 119, 120, 129, 137, 139, 140, 141, 143, and 149.

These expressions of rage and demands for justice are so prevalent and harshly worded that they cannot be easily ignored or dismissed. And they're not limited to the Psalms; we also see these types of prayers in the laments of Jeremiah and Habakkuk.

There are a few different ways that Christians have tried to come to terms with these types of prayers in the Psalms. Some have said that they are sinful expressions of inconsolable rage and that we should avoid these types of prayers at all costs. Others have said that David and the other psalmists are just exaggerating or that these prayers are simply describing what will *eventually* happen to these evildoers sometime in the eternal state. Others have argued that because these prayers were offered "under law," they are no longer relevant to those of us who are now "under grace." In light of Jesus' teaching about praying for our enemies, these arguments may seem compelling until we read this type of prayer in the book of Revelation, prayed by the *glorified* saints under the altar:

When he opened the fifth seal, I saw under the altar the souls of those who had been slain because of the word of God and the testimony they had maintained. They called out in a loud voice, *"How long, Sovereign Lord, holy and true, until you judge the inhabitants of the earth and avenge our blood?"* Then each of them was given a white robe, and they were told to wait a little longer, until the full number of their fellow servants, their brothers and sisters, were killed just as they had been. (Revelation 6:9-11, emphasis added)

Are these saints just exaggerating? No, they really want God to act on their behalf. Are they sinning in their prayer? No, because they've been glorified. Can we say they're under law but not under grace? Certainly not, for the same reason.

So what do we, as believers, *do* with these prayers?

It's best to view the imprecatory psalms as we do the rest of the psalms: as deep, heartfelt expressions that we offer to the throne of heaven, confident that God will not only comfort us (as He did the martyred saints in Revelation 6) but also give us the confidence that He will have the final word in all matters of injustice. Then we will be free to forgive our enemies and eventually be able to ask God to be merciful to them, even if they remain hard-hearted and remorseless.[2]

You will learn more about these prayers in lesson 5.

Can Prayer Really Make a Difference?

As you will discover in this study, the book of Psalms is a collection of prayers offered to us as examples to follow. But even so, some people struggle with the concept of prayer. If God determines everything, they reason, why bother? No one has answered this question better than the great statesman of the church C. S. Lewis:

> Can we believe that God ever really modifies His action in response to the suggestions of man? For infinite wisdom does not need telling what is best, and infinite goodness needs no urging to do it. But neither does God need any of those things that are done by finite agents, whether living or inanimate. He could, if He chose, repair our bodies miraculously without food; or give us food without the aid of farmers, bakers, and butchers; or knowledge without the aid of learned men; or convert the heathen without missionaries. Instead, He allows soils and weather and animals and the muscles, minds, and wills of men to cooperate in the execution of His will. "God," says Pascal, "instituted prayer in order to lend to His creatures the dignity of causality." But it is not only prayer; whenever we act at all, He lends us that dignity. It is not really stranger, nor less strange, that my prayers should affect the course of events than that my other actions should do so.
>
> C. S. Lewis, *The Efficacy of Prayer*

May the Lord richly bless your study of the Psalms as you and those in your small group learn to pray in a way that touches the heart of God.

1. Frank E. Gaebelein, ed., *The Expositor's Bible Commentary*, vol. 5 (Grand Rapids, MI: Zondervan, 1991).
2. Doug Schmidt, *The Prayer of Revenge: Forgiveness in the Face of Injustice* (Colorado Springs, CO: Cook, 2003).

PRAYERS OF WORSHIP AND PRAISE

Ascribe to the LORD, you heavenly beings, ascribe to
the LORD glory and strength. Ascribe to the LORD
the glory due his name. (Psalm 29:1-2)

Lesson Objective: That participants will understand
how worship and praise is foundational to effective
and satisfying times of prayer.

Desired Action: That participants would approach
times of prayer with an attitude of reverence and
awe for God.

Psalms for This Lesson: 19, 24, 29, 33, 34, 47, 48,
65, 66, 67, 76, 89, 92, 93, 96, 97, 98, 100, 104, 108,
117, 122, 134, 147, 148, 149, 150

Psalms are typically associated with praise and worship. Many contemporary praise choruses are simply
the psalms set to modern music. In fact, this reflects
the original purpose of many of the psalms: to be
sung in order to prepare people's hearts for worship
in the temple. In this sense, they can also prepare
our hearts for prayer, for it is only in the context of
worship that prayers of confession, intercession, and
thanksgiving have any meaning at all. When we
focus on the power, greatness, and majesty of God,
everything else is placed in its proper perspective.

For Thought and Discussion: What effect has nature had on your perception of God? Are you moved by a beautiful sunset or a majestic animal in the wild? Does your view of God change when nature becomes violent and seemingly out of control? What is the weather like right now? Of which part of God's character does today's climate remind you?

Psalm 19:1-6

For the director of music. A psalm of David.

The heavens declare the glory of God;
    the skies proclaim the work of his hands.
Day after day they pour forth speech;
    night after night they reveal knowledge.
They have no speech, they use no words;
    no sound is heard from them.
Yet their voice goes out into all the earth,
    their words to the ends of the world.
In the heavens God has pitched a tent for the sun.
    It is like a bridegroom coming out of his
        chamber,
    like a champion rejoicing to run his course.
It rises at one end of the heavens
    and makes its circuit to the other;
    nothing is deprived of its warmth.

1. *The heavens declare the glory of God; the skies proclaim the work of his hands (19:1).* What are some ways that nature provokes you to worship the Creator? What are some of your favorite outdoor places to pray?

    _____

    _____

    _____

    _____

2. *They have no speech, they use no words; no sound is heard from them. Yet their voice goes out into all the earth, their words to the ends of the world. (19:3-4).* Imagine people in different countries seeing the same beautiful night sky and being moved to prayer in different languages. What is it about praying with brothers and sisters around the world that is so exciting even though we might not speak the same language?

    _____

    _____

_____

_____

3. Why should prayer be at the heart of worship? Is it possible to worship without prayer? Explain.

_____

_____

_____

_____

Pavilion. The bridegroom's pavilion would have been a covered place, such as a booth or small tent, where the groom would have been kept in waiting for the bride. The purpose was to make his entrance into the wedding that much more spectacular.

Psalm 19:7-8

The law of the LORD is perfect,
   refreshing the soul.
The statutes of the LORD are trustworthy,
   making wise the simple.
The precepts of the LORD are right,
   giving joy to the heart.
The commands of the LORD are radiant,
   giving light to the eyes.

4. *The law of the LORD is perfect (19:7)*. What role should the Bible play in our worship? How is studying the Bible in depth different from using the Scriptures during a time of worship?

_____

_____

_____

_____

Optional Application: Take a hike along a nature trail. Use the things you see along the path as prompts for your prayers. If you see a sparrow, thank God for His provision. If you see a tree along a stream, thank God for His Living Water that replenishes your soul. If you swat a mosquito, thank God for the patience to endure and forgive difficult people. Praise God for the warmth of the sun or the coolness of the breeze.

For Further Study: Do a quick online study of astronomy. What do the exact and consistent orbits of the galaxies tell us about the levels and depths of God's intelligence and power as the Creator of the literal universe?

For Thought and Discussion: How has your view of the Bible changed over the years? Why is it important to view it as the authoritative Word of God rather than simply another famous book?

Optional Application: Write a letter to your pastor, thanking him or her for faithfully proclaiming the Word of God every week so that your soul is fed.

For Further Study: Look up *general revelation* in a theological dictionary. How does this differ from *special revelation*? Do you think there's enough "general revelation" out there so that every person can be held accountable by God even if he or she has never been exposed to "special revelation"? Explain.

5. *Refreshing the soul . . . making wise the simple . . . giving joy to the heart . . . giving light to the eyes (19:7-8).* What have the practical manifestations of these benefits from God's Word looked like in your life?

_____

_____

_____

_____

6. How does the faithful preaching of God's Word affect how you pray or what you pray about?

_____

_____

_____

_____

Laws, statutes, precepts, and commands. In contrast to the general revelation of God in nature, the special revelation of God through His Word is focused and far less prone to subjective interpretation. Whereas the general revelation of God points to His intelligence and existence, the specific revelation of God tells us how He wants us to live.

Psalm 19:9-11

The fear of the LORD is pure,
  enduring forever.
The decrees of the LORD are firm,
  and all of them are righteous.
They are more precious than gold,
  than much pure gold;
they are sweeter than honey,
  than honey from the honeycomb.
By them your servant is warned;
  in keeping them there is great reward.

7. *The fear of the* Lord *is pure, enduring forever (19:9).* How do we express our "fear of God" in prayer? Is this more than reverence? Explain.

_____

_____

_____

_____

8. *By them is your servant warned; in keeping them there is great reward (19:11).* What does God's Word command of us in regard to prayer? What are the consequences of ignoring these commands? What are the great benefits of faithful and consistent prayer?

_____

_____

_____

_____

_____

_____

_____

9. Who were some of the great pray-ers in the Bible whose examples we can follow?

_____

_____

_____

For Thought and Discussion: Which motivates you more: the fear of loss or the anticipation of reward? How do you see both of these motivations at work in your life?

Optional Application: List some of the great ways your life has benefited because you respect what the Word of God says and you've obeyed it. How would your life be different if you didn't take the Bible seriously?

For Further Study: How often Is the prospect of reward mentioned in the Bible? Is it mentioned enough for us to think that it's okay for the Christian to be motivated by reward? What is the better motivator: the anticipation of reward or the fear of loss?

Honey from the honeycomb. The *tsuph* was made up of the cells of a honeycomb that were filled with honey; although the cells were not edible, you could put the *tsuph* in your mouth as a utensil for the honey. These types of combs occurred naturally, usually in forested areas, and were considered a delicacy for the weary traveler.

For Thought and Discussion: Why is it important to realize that God is never "contributing to the problem" when it comes to aspects of our relationship with Him that need work?

Psalm 19:12-14

But who can discern their own errors?
    Forgive my hidden faults.
Keep your servant also from willful sins;
    may they not rule over me.
Then will I be blameless,
    innocent of great transgression.

May these words of my mouth and this meditation of
        my heart
    be pleasing in your sight,
    O LORD, my Rock and my Redeemer.

10. *Keep your servant also from willful sins (19:13).*
    What is the difference between willful sin and
    sin done in ignorance? How should we confess
    them differently in prayer?

    _____

    _____

    _____

    _____

    _____

11. *May these words of my mouth and this
    meditation of my heart be pleasing in your
    sight (19:14).* What is it about our thoughts and
    prayers during worship that delights the heart of
    God?

    _____

    _____

    _____

    _____

    _____

12. Why is a clean heart and conscience necessary
    for effective worship?

    _____

    _____

_____

_____

Rule over me. The compelling, addictive power of sin was no less intense during the time of David than it is today. Whether our sin is an addiction to a substance or destructive behavior, the psalmist reminds us that only the power of God can set us free from the entanglement of our sin

---

For the group

Warm-up. Ask your group members about some of their expectations for this particular study. Is there anything in particular they want to learn about prayer? Do they simply want to become more consistent in their prayer life? Do they have questions about whether prayer really makes a difference? Do they understand that most of the psalms are prayers themselves and that there is much we can learn from them? Be sure to write down their responses and find the part in the study where those questions will be addressed.

Questions. Psalm 19 is representative of a host of psalms that focus on the worship and praise of God. While the questions in this lesson are derived from Psalm 19, they illustrate the biblical principles that are part of any expression of worship to God. This psalm focuses on the value of the Word in worship and why God's revelation is such an intricate part of the biblical experience of praise. Some of the questions will help you better understand the views of the Bible held by your group. Those members who do not see the Bible as a reliable and authoritative source of God's truth are going to have a hard time with the rest of the study. If they need special attention in this area, be sure they get it — either through you, a pastor, or perhaps a special class at church.

Prayer. Set the tone for the entire study by offering nothing but expressions of praise and worship of God during the closing time of prayer. Everything else you're going to study is based on this. So much of prayer involves acknowledging different attributes of

Optional Application: Describe a possible ongoing grievance between yourself and a friend or family member and assign "percentages" of blame to each person. How is the other person contributing to the problem? How much are you? What can you do this week to take care of your percentage?

For Further Study: Study the concept of "redeemer" in the book of Ruth. How does the example of Boaz help us understand God as Redeemer?

19

God. If we focus on these attributes during times of worship, our times spent in the types of prayer you'll study in the coming weeks will be far richer and more colorful.

PRAYERS OF CONFESSION AND ACKNOWLEDGMENT

Blessed is the one whose transgressions are forgiven,
whose sins are covered. (Psalm 32:1)

Lesson Objective: That participants will understand the importance of internalizing responsibility for personal sins.

Desired Action: That participants will immediately confess and acknowledge their sin in prayer when they experience genuine guilt, in order to resolve any lingering sense of shame and be fully reconciled with God.

Psalms for This Lesson: 6, 15, 32, 38, 51, 88, 123, 130, 143

The psalms of confession, or the *penitential psalms*, are attributed to King David. We can be certain that all of them reflect an emotional response to the king's recently uncovered disobedience. Psalm 51 was written after Nathan confronted David about his adultery with Bathsheba. Other psalms might be in response to the king's disobedient demand for a census, or sins of David for which we have no record. These prayers express the writer's deeply felt acknowledgment and contrition over personal sin and we see what genuine repentance looks like. As Peter tells us, unconfessed sin in our relationships will hinder our prayers (see 1 Peter 3:7). By following David's

Optional Application:
Privately make a list of this week's sins of commission and omission (sinful words, thoughts, and actions you actually said, had, or did, and sins you committed by not doing something). Next to each one, write an excuse as to why you did it or did not do it. After each excuse, describe why that excuse is not legitimate. (Note: If an action can be rightly excused, then it's not sinful.)

For Thought and Discussion:
What is the relationship between acknowledging we've done something wrong and our ability to be reconciled with the people who were affected by our sin? Is reconciliation between people even possible without such acknowledgment? Can anyone be reconciled with God without confession? Explain.

example of confessing, such hindrances to our prayers can be removed.

1. *The forgiven are blessed (Psalm 32:1).* Why is it not possible to have a sense of well-being when we're aware of unconfessed sin in our lives?

_____

_____

_____

_____

2. How is refusing to internalize responsibility for sin a form of self-deceit (see 32:2)?

_____

_____

_____

_____

3. *A physical response to unconfessed sin (32:3-4).* What could be a modern medical explanation for the symptoms David describes in these verses?

_____

_____

_____

4. How is it that what happens in the mind can affect the body so dramatically?

_____

_____

_____

5. *A detailed confession (32:5).* Why is it important to be specific about what we've done that was wrong and about the damage it caused to ourselves and others?

_____

_____

_____

_____

6. *Asking for mercy (51:1-2).* Why does it sometimes seem that even after a detailed confession, promises not to repeat the behavior, and pledges to make restitution, we still feel empty and unforgiven?

_____

_____

_____

_____

7. In cases like these, why is asking for mercy the only viable option left? Why did Jesus say that the tax collector's crying out, "God, have mercy on me, a sinner!" justified him before God (see Luke 18:9-14)?

_____

_____

_____

_____

8. *The role of guilt (51:3).* What is the role of guilt as an emotional response to sin?

_____

_____

_____

_____

9. Why is guilt often seen as an illegitimate emotion, something to be avoided or downplayed at all costs? What God-honoring purpose can guilt fulfill?

For Thought and Discussion: In Psalm 32, David seems to have experienced God's forgiveness. In Psalm 51 (written after being confronted about his sin with Bathseba), David seems to be waiting for God's forgiveness. What would account for the difference?

For Further Study: Read Psalms 6 and 38. Compare some of the physical responses to unconfessed sin that you read in these prayers with those described in Psalm 32. It's important to note that these psalms are written in response to legitimate guilt. Many people are plagued by a sense of ambiguous guilt that they cannot tie to any specific immoral action. Legitimate guilt serves a purpose similar to that of physical pain in the body: It tells us something's wrong and needs to be acknowledged. So, in this sense, guilt should never be a lingering emotion; whatever is causing it should be given immediate attention.

Optional Application: How long are you usually willing to tolerate feeling guilty before you just own up to what you did that's causing the painful emotion? What kinds of things cause your guilt to linger? How can you decisively deal with that situation so that the guilt really goes away?

_____

_____

_____

_____

_____

10. Read John 16:7-9. What is the role of the Holy Spirit in convicting us of sin? How does His influence help us distinguish between legitimate and illegitimate guilt?

_____

_____

_____

_____

11. When does legitimate guilt become unhealthy?

_____

_____

_____

_____

_____

12. *Sinning against God (Psalm 51:4).* Why is any sin we commit considered a sin *only* against God?

_____

_____

_____

_____

_____

13. Does this free us from acknowledging our sin to those who were affected by our sin? Are there

times when confessing our sins to someone else can do more harm than good? Explain.

_____

_____

_____

_____

_____

Conceived in sin. "Surely I was sinful at birth, sinful from the time my mother conceived me" (51:5). Medieval theologians often referred to this verse to support the idea that all sex, even solely for the purpose of procreation, is in some way sinful. What the psalmist is really trying to say here is that there was never a point in his human existence when he did not have a "bent" toward sin, even in the womb. Many conservative theologians see this expression as supporting the idea of original sin as it mysteriously passed down to all human beings from our fallen first parents, Adam and Eve.

Hyssop. "Cleanse me with hyssop, and I will be clean" (51:7). Hyssop is an aromatic, semi-woody plant with fine hairs at the tips of its branches. It is indigenous to Northern Africa and Western Asia and was used by the Israelites to brush the lamb's blood over their doorposts during the first Passover in Egypt. Because of that event, hyssop came to be associated with blood-covered protection from sin. The plant was also used to give Jesus vinegar on the cross.

14. *God's desire for inward truth (51:6).* Why is it so freeing to simply acknowledge what is factually true when it comes to our sinful decisions?

_____

_____

_____

_____

25

15. Why does blaming circumstances or other people (for our sin) to keep us "shielded" from the truth require so much energy?

_____

_____

_____

_____

16. Why is the exceptional pain of acknowledging sin better to experience than the delayed (but excruciating) pain of keeping sin covered up?

_____

_____

_____

_____

Bit and bridle. "Do not be like the horse or the mule, which have no understanding but must be controlled by bit and bridle" (32:9). The horse bit is a metal bar placed in the interdental part of the animal's mouth (where there are no teeth). The bridle is usually made up of leather strips to hold the bit in place. By pulling to one side or the other, the horse is compelled to turn in that direction to prevent further discomfort from the bit. The psalmist's point is that unconfessed sin is like an uncomfortable bit in our mouth that compels us to go in a direction we don't want to go. Of course, the psalmist doesn't want us to miss the "stubborn mule" part of this metaphor either.

17. *A pure heart (51:10-12).* What are the spiritual benefits of fully acknowledging our sin before God? What prevents many believers from experiencing these benefits?

_____

_____

_____

_____

_____

18. *The only sacrifice for sin (51:16-17)*. What kinds of sacrifices do some people like to make instead of confessing their sin? Why is this type of self-appointed "atonement" always ineffective?

_____

_____

_____

_____

_____

For the group

Warm-up. Ask your group what they think about people who "plead the fifth amendment" when they're in the courtroom and don't want to incriminate themselves. Have them discuss the ways people "plead the fifth" outside of the courtroom and the impact that can have on their credibility.

Questions. Confession is one of those topics that people are often hesitant to talk about in a group. Quite often, public confession is inappropriate. That's why some of the application activities are to be done privately. Whenever possible, try to talk about these things in the "third person." For example, ask, "Why do some people find it difficult to own up to what they've done wrong?" instead of "Why do *you* find it difficult to own up to what you've done wrong?" The answers group members give will likely reflect how they would personally answer the question; this just gives them a "safe" way to do that.

The goal of this lesson is to get participants to internalize responsibility for personal sins and then to express that sense of "ownership" in prayer. Second, if their sin has caused a rift in one of their relationships, they will be encouraged to acknowledge responsibility for what they did to the person

Optional Application: Privately describe how some of your relationships have been affected by sin, either your own or someone else's. What kinds of things would have to be acknowledged for the relationship to get back on track and perhaps even deepen?

For Thought and Discussion: What is it about sin that erodes trust between people? Why must sin be acknowledged for trust to be regained? What does it mean to be trusted by someone (namely, God) from whom we can hide nothing? Why does God want us to acknowledge what He can plainly see is true?

they hurt. This way, the door of reconciliation might be opened and the confessor's prayers no longer hindered.

However, there are instances when confessing sins to someone will do more harm than good—for instance, harboring jealousy toward someone because of his or her economic status. If the person doesn't know he or she has been sinned against, that person probably doesn't need to know.

Prayer. Focus the closing prayer on asking God for the courage to confess and acknowledge sin. There are few human experiences more emotionally painful than owning up to something we've done out of malice or negligence. However, once we've swallowed this bitter pill and confessed, we are free to experience the grace of God and reconciled relationships.

PRAYERS OF INTERCESSION AND SUPPLICATION

In the morning, LORD, you hear my voice; in
the morning I lay my requests before you
and wait expectantly. (Psalm 5:3)

Lesson Objective: That participants will understand
that God expects us to frequently ask Him for what
we want and need.

Desired Action: That participants will be specific
and persistent in their requests to God on behalf of
themselves and others and will trust God to fulfill,
deny, or provide alternatives to their requests as He
sees fit.

Psalms for This Lesson: 5, 21, 91, 102, 113, 115,
121, 146

Many of the psalms are quite bold about our need
to present our requests to God. Quite often these
requests are included in the psalms of lament or
deliverance. In the New Testament (especially in
James), there is an emphasis on the human motivations behind making our requests. In the psalms
studied in this lesson, we see a greater emphasis on
God's motivation for responding to and answering
our prayers of request.

Psalm 5:1-3

Listen to my words, LORD,
    consider my lament.
Hear my cry for help,
    my King and my God,
    for to you I pray.
In the morning, LORD, you hear my voice;
    in the morning I lay my requests before you
    and wait expectantly.

1. *In the morning, LORD, you hear my voice (5:3).* Why is it important to start the day talking with God? Is there any reason why that conversation needs to stop as the day progresses? Explain.

_____

_____

_____

_____

2. *I lay my requests before you (5:3).* In what ways is laying our requests before God like making a presentation? What kind of preparation should this type of prayer involve?

_____

_____

_____

_____

3. *[I] wait expectantly (5:3).* Why should we have a sense of expectation after we pray? How does that sense of expectation reflect our faith? Should we pray anyway, even if expectations are low and faith is ebbing? Explain.

_____

_____

_____

_____

_____

_____

_____

_____

The kingship of God. In the Psalms, Yahweh is frequently portrayed as the past and present king, especially by King David. In the psalms of lament (such as Psalm 5), when God is addressed as King, he is seen as the Divine Monarch, who alone has the ability to deliver His people and fulfill their requests. In the Psalms, God is the everlasting, sustaining, and judging King.

Psalm 21:1-2

For the director of music. A psalm of David.

The king rejoices in your strength, LORD.
How great is his joy in the victories you give!
You have granted him his heart's desire
and have not withheld the request of his lips.

4. *The king rejoices in your strength, LORD (21:1).* What is it about the strength and power of God that gives us the confidence to bring our requests to Him?

_____

_____

_____

_____

_____

5. *How great is his joy in the victories you give! (21:1).* What is it about past "victories" (crystal-

Optional Application: Make a two-column chart. In the left column, list your requests of God for the week. In the right column, describe how you expect God to answer your prayer. Are there some requests for which you are more confident about receiving a yes from God? What is special about those requests compared to the others?

For Further Study: Look up these famous "Yes" answers to prayer: Moses prays for Pharaoh (see Exodus 8:12-13), Hannah prays for a baby (see 1 Samuel 1:10-11), Solomon prays for his nation (see 1 Kings 8:22-61), Elijah prays for rain (see James 5:17), Elisha prays for his servant (see 2 Kings 6:17), Hezekiah prays for healing (see 2 Kings 20:1-11). Why do you think God said yes to these prayer requests?

For Thought and Discussion: Why does Psalm 21 apply to "non-kings" as well as to the monarch described here?

31

Optional Application: Make a list of your lifetime "Top Three" answers to prayer. Try to recall how you felt when God miraculously intervened on your behalf.

For Further Study: Look up these famous "No" answers to prayer: Paul prays for his thorn to be removed (see 2 Corinthians 12:8), Jesus prays for his cup to be removed (see Matthew 26:39). Why do you think God declined these requests?

clear answers to prayer) that gives us confidence to bring our requests to Him?

_____

_____

_____

_____

6. *You have granted him his heart's desire . . . the request of his lips (21:2).* If the king had not made these requests, would there be anything to praise God about? Explain. What is it about fulfilled prayer requests that compels us to worship God?

_____

_____

_____

_____

_____

_____

God rules through the human king. While some psalms focus on God's kingship, prayers such as Psalm 21 focus on how God works through the human kings He appoints. Some scholars believe that this psalm contains part of a royal liturgy that would have been spoken at a king's inauguration.

Psalm 91:14-16

"Because he loves me," says the LORD, "I will rescue him;
    I will protect him, for he acknowledges my name.
He will call on me, and I will answer him;
    I will be with him in trouble,
    I will deliver him and honor him.
With long life will I satisfy him
    and show him my salvation."

7. *"Because he loves me," says the* LORD, *"I will rescue him (91:14).* Why are we compelled to do things for people who love and care about us? What is it about our love for God that motivates Him to answer our prayers?

_____

_____

_____

_____

_____

_____

For Thought and Discussion: Describe the two-way interaction we read here in Psalm 91. What do we do? What does God do in response?

8. *He will call on me, and I will answer him (91:15).* According to this passage, if we cry out, "God, are you there?" how will He respond? How does this impact your motivation to seek out God and present your requests to Him?

_____

_____

_____

_____

_____

_____

9. *With long life will I satisfy him (91:16).* If someone dies at a relatively young age, does this mean he or she wasn't being heard by God? Explain.

_____

_____

_____

_____

_____

Optional Application: Count the ways you love God. Consider the ways you express your love for Him in every area of your life. How do you think God feels about your affection for Him?

For Further Study: Read about Job's prayer for his friends in Job 42. Why did God command Job to pray for those who were essentially taunting him during a very difficult period? How did God deliver and honor Job, as described in Psalm 91?

For Thought and Discussion: What are some of life's truly desperate situations that people always bring to prayer? What is it about a truly distressed plea that compels God to come to that person's aid?

The shelter of the Most High. The psalmist makes use of metaphors to illustrate the power of God to protect and provide refuge. The words *shelter* and *shadow* are often used in reference to the ways birds protect their young, which brings to mind Jesus' wish for Jerusalem: that He might take them under His wings as a hen does her chicks (see Matthew 23:37; Luke 13:34).

Psalm 102:16-17

For the LORD will rebuild Zion
    and appear in his glory.
He will respond to the prayer of the destitute;
    he will not despise their plea.

10. *He will respond to the prayer of the destitute (102:17).* How do you distinguish between the poor (as described in Scripture) and those who have no money because they refuse to work or feel entitled to the support of others?

_____

_____

_____

_____

11. Why would you think God is more inclined to respond to the prayers of the one over the other?

_____

_____

_____

_____

12. *He will not despise their plea (102:17).* Why do some people feel uncomfortable about requests for help from needy people? Why is this particular issue not a problem for God?

_____

_____

_____

_____

_____

For the group

Warm-up. Ask for volunteers to talk about their comfort level when it comes to making requests of others. In the corporate environment, it may come naturally, as people at work are asked to do things all the time. But is it different when the request can be voluntarily fulfilled or denied? How about when it will cost the person whom we're asking to fulfill our request? Who is it easiest to ask for things? Family? Friends? Your church? God?

Questions. Many of this lesson's questions focus on God's desire and willingness to listen to our requests and to fulfill those requests (or not) according to His sovereign will. Many Christians feel that they're imposing on others when they make requests, and this can carry over into their prayers to God.

So much is written about the Christian's motivation when it comes to making requests of God. Often our motivation is presented as the "toggle switch" that lights up the "yes" or "no" bulbs determining whether God will grant a request. In this study, there is less emphasis on the human-intention side of things. Instead, encourage group members to boldly ask God for what they think God wants for them and let the Holy Spirit work on the integrity of their motivation.

Prayer. Before going to prayer, read these passages from the New Testament about the importance of offering up prayers of intercession and supplication. Note how seamlessly these Scriptures fit with the Psalms that focus on making requests to God, whether on behalf of ourselves or others.

> Pray in the Spirit on all occasions with all kinds of prayers and requests. With this in mind, be alert and always keep on praying for all the Lord's people. (Ephesians 6:18)
>
> I urge, then, first of all, that petitions, prayers, intercession and thanksgiving be made for all people —

35

for kings and all those in authority, that we may live
peaceful and quiet lives in all godliness and holiness.
(1 Timothy 2:1-2)

Do not be anxious about anything, but in every
situation, by prayer and petition, with thanksgiving,
present your requests to God. (Philippians 4:6)

Ask people for specific prayer requests and write them down. Make sure everyone's request is presented to God during this closing prayer. Focus less on our motivation and emphasize God's ability and willingness to answer our prayers. God simply wants us to articulate, to Him, what is on our hearts and what we believe we need.

PRAYERS OF PROTECTION AND DELIVERANCE

In you, O LORD, I have taken refuge; let me
never be put to shame; deliver me in
your righteousness. (Psalm 31:1)

Lesson Objective: That participants will understand the importance of placing their sense of ultimate security in no one else but God.

Desired Action: That participants will seek the Lord during times of impending and actual trouble, trusting Him to keep them from difficult circumstances or to help them to endure those trials if they come.

Psalms for This Lesson: 3, 8, 11, 12, 16, 18, 20, 25, 28, 30, 31, 35, 40, 46, 52, 59, 61, 69, 70, 71, 116, 124, 129, 140, 142, 143

The psalms of protection and deliverance are almost all based on historical events in the writers' lives. Nowhere in Scripture do we find a stronger precedent for praying out of and through our life's experiences. This is where the raw materials of prayer are forged, and sometimes when such prayers are expressed, the words are a bit rough and the thoughts a bit disorganized. No matter. Regardless of our ability to think clearly, we must pray in the midst of crisis. We can be confident that the Holy Spirit will filter, interpret, and express our thoughts perfectly to the heavenly throne.

37

In these psalms, we read the thoughts and prayers of people who have hit rock bottom—or at least rock bottom is staring them in the face. But the triumphant refrain of these psalms is that God is as powerful in the valley and at the bottom of the seas as He is at the mountaintops of our lives.

Psalm 28:1-2

Of David.

> To you, LORD, I call;
> > you are my Rock,
> > do not turn a deaf ear to me.
> For if you remain silent,
> > I will be like those who go down to the pit.
> Hear my cry for mercy
> > as I call to you for help,
> as I lift up my hands
> > toward your Most Holy Place.

1. *If you remain silent, I will be like those who go down to the pit (28:1).* Why does it often seem, in the middle of a crisis, that God appears to go "silent"? Is there something about a trial that affects our ability to sense God's presence? Explain your answers.

   _____

   _____

   _____

   _____

   _____

2. *Hear my cry for mercy as I call to you for help (28:2).* Why do you think the Psalms hold nothing back when it comes to expressing deep emotions in prayer? Why should we tell God how we feel if He knows already?

   _____

   _____

_____

_____

_____

_____

3. Why is God the "safest" person to hear and receive our deepest fears and concerns? How does expressing those emotions in prayer, to a God who is completely sovereign, help us process those feelings?

_____

_____

_____

_____

_____

Most Holy Place. The Most Holy Place was that part of the temple most closely associated with the presence of God. Here the ark of the covenant was placed, guarded by the golden cherubim. The Most Holy Place gave the psalmist great inner strength when he appealed to God for deliverance.

Psalm 3:1-4

A psalm of David. When he fled from his son Absalom.

LORD, how many are my foes!
    How many rise up against me!
Many are saying of me,
    "God will not deliver him."
But you, LORD, are a shield around me,
    my glory, the One who lifts my head high.
I call out to the LORD,
    and he answers me from his holy mountain.

4. *You, LORD, are a shield around me (3:3).* What types of things do we need to be shielded from

Optional Application: Take a vow of silence for a day. Let the people in your inner circle know what's going on. Keep track of what you want to communicate to others, but choose not to (for the day). Do you think God ever takes a temporary vow of silence with us? If so, why do you think He would do that?

For Further Study: Read the account of David's flight from Saul in 1 Samuel 23–24. (This is the historical context of Psalm 28.) Why would Saul's relentless pursuit generate such despair in the young man?

For Thought and Discussion: What often happens to our friendships during times of crisis? What kind of "filtering" effects often occur to those relationships? What characteristics of true friends seem to rise to the surface when we need them most?

39

Optional Application: Find somebody in crisis this week and encourage that person with a call or e-mail. It would be especially good if you can find someone who is going through something difficult that you've survived. Be ready if the person wishes to extend the discussion.

For Further Study: Read the account of David's flight from Absalom in 2 Samuel 15–17. Why would this flight from his own son be so much more emotionally gut-wrenching than fleeing from Saul was? What did David learn about God from his first fugitive experience that helped him with this one?

during a difficult trial? What difference does it make when God acts as this shield?

_____

_____

_____

_____

_____

5. *I call out to the LORD, and he answers me from his holy mountain (3:4).* Why does it sometimes help to verbalize our prayers aloud? If we didn't think God was ever going to answer our prayers, what would happen to our motivation to pray?

_____

_____

_____

_____

6. Why is prayer the best defense against those who are pessimistic or antagonistic toward those in crisis? How does prayer help when well-intentioned people offer their hopeless prognoses?

_____

_____

_____

_____

The first psalm. Psalm 3 is the first psalm attributed to David. It is also the first of thirteen psalms attributed, in the Psalter, to a particular episode in David's life. (The other twelve psalms are 7, 18, 34, 51, 52, 54, 56, 57, 59, 60, 63, 142).

40

As in the other psalms of crisis, we see David's confidence in the power and sovereignty of God, despite human stupidity.

Psalm 18:1-3

For the director of music. Of David the servant of the LORD. He sang to the LORD the words of this song when the LORD delivered him from the hand of all his enemies and from the hand of Saul. He said:

> I love you, O LORD, my strength.
> The LORD is my rock, my fortress and my deliverer;
>   my God is my rock, in whom I take refuge,
>   my shield and the horn of my salvation, my
>   stronghold.
> I called to the LORD, who is worthy of praise,
>   and I have been saved from my enemies.

7. *The LORD is my rock, my fortress and my deliverer (18:2).* Why is shelter the first thing we look for when caught in the storm? How does God fulfill this role during the times of squalor in our lives?

_____

_____

_____

_____

_____

8. *I called to the LORD . . . and I have been saved from my enemies (18:3).* Why do some Christians tend to believe they don't have any real enemies? Why are they often caught off guard by the deliberately destructive behavior of people who have declared war on the kingdom of God and those who belong to it?

_____

_____

_____

For Thought and Discussion: What do enemies look like today? Do they have any distinctive physical or emotional traits? What do they have in common?

41

Optional Application: Create a physical space for yourself that you can consider a "sanctuary." It might be the corner of a room or a quiet place in the forest. While you are there, thank God for being your refuge, a source of peace you can tap into during any storm.

For Further Study: Look at the story of Job again and notice if he responded any differently to the consequences of the natural versus moral evil in his life. Did he view God as less sovereign over one than the other? Explain. In God's speech to Job, how did He demonstrate his sovereignty over every natural and moral force in the universe?

_____

_____

_____

_____

9. What is the difference between crises caused by "natural evil" (health, hurricanes, and so on) and those that come out of "moral evil" (for example, the malice of others)? How should we pray differently in these situations?

_____

_____

_____

_____

Many enemies. The inscription of Psalm 18 includes other enemies of David besides Saul. This could have included the Philistines, Goliath, Nabal, and many others. What's unique here is that we see how David trusts in God the same way in the midst of similar circumstances. David was master of gaining confidence in the Lord's future deliverance by looking back at the many times God rescued him.

Psalm 31:1-3

For the director of music. A psalm of David.

In you, LORD, I have taken refuge;
    let me never be put to shame;
    deliver me in your righteousness.
Turn your ear to me,
    come quickly to my rescue;
be my rock of refuge,
    a strong fortress to save me.
Since you are my rock and my fortress,
    for the sake of your name lead and guide me.

10. *Let me never be put to shame (31:1).* Why do we fear humiliation? What is it about the prospects of shame that drives us to prayer?

_____

_____

_____

_____

_____

11. *Turn your ear to me, come quickly to my rescue (31:2).* How do we know that God is paying attention to us? From what do we often ask to be rescued?

_____

_____

_____

_____

_____

12. *For the sake of your name lead and guide me (31:3).* How does the kingdom's cause benefit when God delivers us from difficult circumstances?

_____

_____

_____

_____

_____

Lament and thanksgiving. Psalm 31 is unique in that it blends two different styles of psalm-writing involving expressions of grief and gratitude. We're never quite sure where the psalmist "lands" emotionally. So it is with our prayers: Sometime we're never quite sure how we feel.

For Thought and Discussion: What are some modern symbols of fortresses? What types of protection do they offer? Do they serve as good analogies to God's protective powers?

Optional Application: Ask the people in your group to share an embarrassing moment. They might not want to share their *most* embarrassing moment, but they might choose one from their top ten. Ask, "What is it about shame that makes it such a powerful emotion, one that most people will do anything to avoid?"

For Further Study: Read the story of Elijah as he was being pursued by Jezebel after the slaughter of her Baal prophets on Mount Carmel (see 1 Kings 19). Elijah probably read Psalm 31 several times in his life. How do you think he responded to David's words during this time of crisis?

Psalm 46:1-3

For the director of music. Of the Sons of Korah. According to alamoth. A song.

> God is our refuge and strength,
>> an ever-present help in trouble.
> Therefore we will not fear, though the earth give way
>> and the mountains fall into the heart of the sea,
> though its waters roar and foam
>> and the mountains quake with their surging.

13. *God is our refuge and strength, an ever-present help in trouble (46:1).* Why do we want God as close to us as possible during troublesome times? How does prayer seem to keep Him there?

_____

_____

_____

_____

_____

14. *Therefore we will not fear (46:2).* How does prayer dissipate the intensity of our fear when there's really something about which to be afraid?

_____

_____

_____

_____

15. In what ways do natural disasters help us understand our lives when they seem to be spinning out of control?

_____

_____

_____

_____

The use of metaphor. Psalm 46 is an excellent example of how the psalmists used word pictures to help us better understand the power and sovereignty of God: refuge, strength, fortress, earthquakes, tidal waves, tsunamis, volcanoes. All of these are similes from nature and man to help us grasp the breadth and depth of God's ability to deliver His people.

For the group

Warm-up. Ask group members to talk about how their view of God changes (if at all) during times of crisis. Sometimes when people are in trouble, they seem to think that God has abandoned them or that they are being punished for something. Help them understand that God's attitude toward us does not change based on our circumstances.

Questions. The psalms of protection and deliverance express some of the deeper emotions of fear and sadness in the Psalms. There are basically five emotions: anger, sadness, happiness, fear, and shame—and, of course, these have many cousins. As the group discusses the questions in this lesson, encourage members to talk about how they feel (using one of the five emotion words) so that they can better relate to the emotional essence of these particular psalms.

Prayer. Be sensitive to group members who are going through a significant crisis. Like many of the psalmists, they might not know how to feel, much less how to express those feelings. Feel for and with them. Hope for and with them. Express this empathy during your time of prayer with them.

Optional Application: Describe the worst storm you've ever experienced. Did you know it was coming? Did you get caught off guard? What kind of shelter were you able to find? What did you learn about yourself after the storm had passed?

For Further Study: Read the book of Jonah. How do you think he would have responded to Psalm 46? (He probably did read it several times during his lifetime.)

PRAYERS OF VINDICATION AND FORGIVENESS

Vindicate me, my God, and plead my cause against
an unfaithful nation. Rescue me from those who are
deceitful and wicked. (Psalm 43:1)

Lesson Objective: That participants will understand that God expects us to express ourselves to
Him from the depth of our souls and that He is big
enough to handle all of our emotions, no matter
how intense.

Desired Action: That participants will express their
frustration to God when they are wronged but will
eventually understand that God will have the final
word on what happened so that they are free to worship and to forgive those who have hurt them.

Psalms for This Lesson: 3, 5, 6, 7, 10, 11, 17, 25, 26,
28, 31, 35, 36, 40, 41, 43, 53, 54, 55, 56, 58, 59, 63,
68, 70, 71, 73, 74, 79, 83, 94, 97, 104, 109, 119, 120,
129, 137, 139, 141

The psalms of cursing, or the imprecatory psalms,
are some of the most difficult Bible passages to
understand. The appeals for justice and vindication
are not rare in this collection; they appear in at least
25 percent of the psalms. What are Christ followers
to do with these raw, emotional expressions, especially in light of Jesus' admonition to bless, and not
curse, our enemies? The value of these psalms is
incalculable, especially when it comes to giving us

For Thought and Discussion: Why does the presence of evil seem like a contradiction to the idea that God is good? Why don't many people believe that both can be true at the same time?

precedents to help us work through how we really feel about those who have hurt us so that we can find the freedom to forgive them.

In this sense, Psalm 73 is an excellent representation of the imprecatory psalms. We see the writer expressing deep levels of bitterness about the success of the wicked until he realizes that God will have the final word in the matter. When the psalmist reaches that point, we sense a new freedom to worship and ultimately to forgive. But we must start at square one, and that is to clearly define the offense and the damage it's caused in our lives. Nowhere do we find a better example of how to do this than what we see in the psalms of vindication and forgiveness.

Psalm 73:1-11

A psalm of Asaph.

> Surely God is good to Israel,
>   to those who are pure in heart.
>
> But as for me, my feet had almost slipped;
>   I had nearly lost my foothold.
> For I envied the arrogant
>   when I saw the prosperity of the wicked.
>
> They have no struggles;
>   their bodies are healthy and strong.
> They are free from common human burdens;
>   they are not plagued by human ills.
> Therefore pride is their necklace;
>   they clothe themselves with violence.
> From their callous hearts comes iniquity;
>   their evil imaginations have no limits.
> They scoff, and speak with malice;
>   with arrogance they threaten oppression.
> Their mouths lay claim to heaven,
>   and their tongues take possession of the earth.
> Therefore their people turn to them
>   and drink up waters in abundance.
> They say, "How would God know?
>   Does the Most High know anything?"

1. *I envied the arrogant when I saw the prosperity of the wicked (73:3).* Why is it so deeply disturbing to see arrogant and insensitive people thriving, especially those who have hurt us or someone we care about? Why is it ironic that we often envy their success?

_____

_____

_____

_____

_____

2. *They say, "How would God know? Does the Most High know anything?" (73:11).* What are some of the overt or more subtle ways that you've seen people challenge God's sovereignty?

_____

_____

_____

_____

3. Why does God allow some wicked people to live carefree lives, while those dedicated to Him often suffer unspeakable evils at the hands of these arrogant wrongdoers? Why are we tempted to call God unjust when we see or experience these situations?

_____

_____

_____

_____

_____

Optional Application: Psalm 73 begins with an affirmation of God's goodness and blessing to Israel. Make a list of the top ten blessings of God in your own life and then rank them according to their importance to you.

For Further Study: Read Pharaoh's arrogant defiance of God in Exodus 5. At the time, Pharaoh was the most powerful man in the world and had nothing but contempt for God. List the ways Pharaoh was prospering on the backs of the Hebrew slaves. Why did his entangled connection with these trappings of prosperity ultimately prove to be the downfall of Egypt?

The "heart" of the matter. There are six references to the "heart" in Psalm 73: "the pure in heart" (verse 1); "callous hearts" (verse 7); "kept my

For Thought and Discussion: What motivates some people to be "good"? Is it simply a matter of conscience? Do some people appear to be good only because it somehow gains them an advantage? Explain.

Optional Application: Make a list of your best personality traits, those parts of your character that reflect a deep level of integrity. Then list the "vice" that represents the moral counterpart of your best character traits. What type of person would you be? How would the people in your life be affected by this "Mr. Hyde" manifestation of your personality? Even if this change did bring you wealth and power, would you still want those things in light of what your closest relationships would be like?

heart pure" (verse 13); "my heart was grieved" (verse 21); "my heart may fail" (verse 26); and "God is the strength of my heart" (verse 26). In all of these instances, the heart represents the place where a person either responds to or rejects God's goodness, embraces or shuns God's truth.

Psalm 73:12-15

This is what the wicked are like—
    always free of care, they go on amassing wealth.

Surely in vain have I kept my heart pure
    and have washed my hands in innocence.
All day long I have been afflicted,
    and every morning brings new punishments.

If I had spoken out like that,
    I would have betrayed your children.

4. *Surely in vain have I kept my heart pure (73:13).* Why does it seem futile to be good when unethical people are able to obtain what we seemingly cannot (because of our unwillingness to morally compromise as they do)?

_____

_____

_____

_____

5. *If I had spoken out like that, I would have betrayed your children (73:15).* How could expressing this kind of bitterness be a stumbling block for other Christians, especially younger ones?

_____

_____

_____

_____

50

6. Do we really want what the wicked have obtained if those things were acquired in shortcut ways that dishonor God? Explain.

_____

_____

_____

_____

Clean hands. "Washed my hands in innocence" is a phrase that also appears in Psalm 26, written by David. The ritual of hand washing, or "ablution," was considered by the Jews to be a rite of purification. The primary biblical basis for this practice is found in Leviticus 15:11, when it was to be done after any kind of "discharge." By performing the act, the faithful person was telling God that he wanted to be pure, in all respects, before Him.

Psalm 73:16-20

When I tried to understand all this,
　　it troubled me deeply
till I entered the sanctuary of God;
　　then I understood their final destiny.

Surely you place them on slippery ground;
　　you cast them down to ruin.
How suddenly are they destroyed,
　　completely swept away by terrors!
They are like a dream when one awakes;
　　when you arise, Lord,
　　you will despise them as fantasies.

7. *Then I understood their final destiny (73:17).* Why was the psalmist able to let go of his bitterness when he understood that God was going to have the final word in the matter that concerned him?

_____

_____

For Further Study: Read the account of the prodigal son in Luke 15:11-32. If the older brother were writing Psalm 73, with the younger brother as "free of care" and "arrogant," what would the older brother write? How would his conclusions be different from Asaph's?

For Thought and Discussion: Contrast these two statements: "Justice delayed is justice denied" with "Justice delayed is still justice." Why is it that waiting for God to hold the wicked accountable can, at times, seem unbearable?

51

Optional Application: List as many "evil people" in history as you can think of (for example, Hitler, Stalin, Pol Pot, Jeffrey Dahmer, Timothy McVeigh). Write a short description of the horrible things they did. Then, if you know, describe how their lives ended. (If you don't know, look it up online). Out of your list, determine how many of these people died in peace, assured that something better awaited them.

For Further Study: Read the account of Korah's demise (and those who followed him) in Numbers 16. Why do you think God isn't causing the earth to "swallow up the wicked" quite as much anymore? How would things be different if God punished every evil act as quickly as He took care of these rebellious people in the wilderness?

8. *Surely you place them on slippery ground; you cast them down to ruin (73:18).* What is it about the inevitable judgment of God that dissipates the desire for revenge and perhaps initiates our ability to forgive?

_____

_____

_____

_____

9. Why did the prospect of such a horrifying end for wrongdoers so radically change the perspective of a person injured by them?

_____

_____

_____

_____

The sanctuary of God. Most likely, this is a reference to the temple. Within the temple, the psalmist gained a sense of the holy presence of God like nowhere else. And so it dawned on him that the wicked could not go on forever, especially in light of God's holiness. A person's evil acts might last a lifetime, but eventually the quality of his or her heart would be tested by God's consuming fire. Only when the psalmist understood this was he able to let go of his bitterness.

Psalm 73:21-28

When my heart was grieved
    and my spirit embittered,
I was senseless and ignorant;
    I was a brute beast before you.

Yet I am always with you;
    you hold me by my right hand.
You guide me with your counsel,
    and afterward you will take me into glory.
Whom have I in heaven but you?
    And earth has nothing I desire besides you.
My flesh and my heart may fail,
    but God is the strength of my heart
    and my portion forever.

Those who are far from you will perish;
    you destroy all who are unfaithful to you.
But as for me, it is good to be near God.
    I have made the Sovereign LORD my refuge;
    I will tell of all your deeds.

For Thought and Discussion: In what sense is the peace of God and the bitterness of long-held grudges mutually incompatible? Why must you give up one in order to have the other?

10. *Whom have I in heaven but you? (73:25).* Why is God "enough" when it comes to dealing with people who have anything but our best interests in mind?

_____

_____

_____

_____

11. *Those who are far from you will perish . . . but as for me, it is good to be near God (73:27-28).* Why doesn't it matter how prosperous someone is if he or she is not reconciled with God?

_____

_____

_____

12. What is it about the presence of God that brings us peace, even in the midst of trials caused by the malice of other people?

_____

_____

_____

53

Optional Application: Make a list of the people in your life around whom you feel the most peaceful. What is it about these folks that is so calming? How can you become more like them?

For Further Study: Read Peter's response to Jesus' offer to the disciples to leave just as the others had done in John 6:66-69. Note why Peter refused to leave: "Lord, to whom shall we go? You have the words of eternal life" (verse 68). Compare this with the response of Asaph in Psalm 73:25.

Glory. The Hebrew word for *glory* used by Asaph (see verse 24) is the same word used to describe the glory of God as it was experienced on Mount Sinai (see Exodus 33:18-23; 34:6-7,29-35). Because God had kept Asaph from sinking into despair and he remained pure of heart, Asaph knew he would experience the blessed presence of God, which would one day cause the wicked to shrink away in terror.

For the group

Warm-up. Start out with a word association game. After you say each word, ask group participants to write down the first word that comes to mind. Then have them write, next to that word, how they feel (using one of the five emotion words: mad, sad, glad, afraid, or ashamed). Here are the words:

- Injustice
- Revenge
- Vindication
- Justice
- Arrogance
- Remorseless
- Forgiving

Ask for volunteers to share their answers. Expect to hear a lot of anger as the primary emotion.

Questions. The psalms of vindication and forgiveness give us a pattern to follow as we work through the forgiveness process. However, many Christians like to skip the hard work of identifying what happened to them and what they lost as a result. Only when they come to terms with these things will they find the freedom to worship and forgive.

Prayer. During your group prayer time, focus on God's sovereignty, acknowledging that He will have the final word in all matters of injustice we've experienced. Also, pray that God would help us hold ourselves to the same standard of acknowledgment that we wish our offenders to respect. We cannot expect others to acknowledge their wrongs if we are unwilling to do so ourselves.

54

PRAYERS OF RENEWAL AND RESTORATION

The LORD is my shepherd, I lack nothing. He makes
me lie down in green pastures, he leads me
beside quiet waters, he refreshes my soul.
He guides me along the right paths for
his name's sake. (Psalm 23:1-3)

Lesson Objective: That participants will see that the
energy they need to live comes from God, as He is
the one who restores and reenergizes us.

Desired Action: That participants will expect and
experience a sense of rest and renewal when they
quiet their hearts before God.

Psalms for This Lesson: 23, 55, 60, 62, 63, 69, 74,
80, 81, 103, 131, 137

For David, prayer was a sanctuary—a place of rest
and restoration. He understood that it was only in
the quiet and still presence of God that his heart
would experience renewal. The classic expression of
this has been Psalm 23, which uses the metaphor
of a loving shepherd to help us understand God's
supreme concern for our souls. As He leads us
beside the still waters, we find rest for our spirits.

For Thought and Discussion: What is it about the human soul that craves "rest"? What can we learn from the body's need for sleep to better understand our inner spirit's need for renewal and restoration?

Optional Application: Try to determine if you are more introverted or extroverted by taking this test:
1. When you arrive for a social event, do you (a) head for the center of the room, or (b) head for somewhere along the wall?
2. Do you feel more energerized after spending time (a) with a friend, or (b) by yourself?
3. Are you (a) hardly ever, or (b) always, distracted by music?
If you have more a's than b's, you're probably extroverted. More b's than a's? Then you're probably introverted. Introverts typically find solitary prayer more satisfying, while extroverts usually would rather pray with someone or in groups.

Psalm 23:1-3

A psalm of David.

The LORD is my shepherd, I lack nothing.
> He makes me lie down in green pastures,
he leads me beside quiet waters,
> he refreshes my soul.
He guides me along the right paths
> for his name's sake.

1. *The LORD is my shepherd, I lack nothing (23:1).* Do you need everything you have? Do you have everything you need? Explain the difference.

   _____

   _____

   _____

   _____

   _____

2. *He refreshes my soul (23:3).* What does your soul feel like when it's restored? How do you know it's in need of restoration?

   _____

   _____

   _____

   _____

   _____

3. Do you feel more energized when you pray by yourself or when you pray with others? What would account for your preference?

   _____

   _____

   _____

   _____

   _____

Shepherd. The first shepherd mentioned in the Bible was Adam and Eve's son Abel. It was out of this labor that Abel presented sacrifices to God. Of course, David was a shepherd, so he has this experience in mind as he unfolds Psalm 23. He understood that sheep trust the shepherd and will listen to only his voice. They know if they listen for his voice, they will be taken to life-sustaining places where they can replenish and rest.

Psalm 23:4

Even though I walk
  through the darkest valley,
I will fear no evil,
  for you are with me;
your rod and your staff,
  they comfort me.

4. *Even though I walk through the darkest valley (23:4).* What does the "darkest valley" seem like to you? What other types of possible "valleys" can drive us to prayer?

_____

_____

_____

_____

_____

_____

5. *I will fear no evil (23:4).* What is it about genuine evil that generates fear? Is God with us only when our fears dissipate, or is He there even when we're in the middle of them?

_____

_____

For Further Study: Contrast the shepherd in Psalm 23 with the ones described in Jude 12: "These people are blemishes at your love feasts, eating with you without the slightest qualm — shepherds who feed only themselves."

For Thought and Discussion: What is it that you fear losing the most? Why does it make sense that the Devil will focus on that thing when he wants to destabilize you? What's your best defense? If you can picture God sustaining you through that particular loss, how would it lose its power over you?

_____

_____

_____

6. Do your prayers always generate a sense of comfort and peace? Why should we pray anyway even if a sense of calm does not come over us?

_____

_____

_____

_____

Rod and staff. Some people have interpreted the rod and staff as instruments of God's discipline, but this does not fit the context of Psalm 23, which is very peaceful and pastoral. In biblical times, the staff was a long stick used to gently keep sheep on the path. The rod was a shorter stick with a weighted end and was used as a weapon to fend off predators. David used both of these when he was a shepherd and here uses the tools to symbolize the comfort that God's direction and protection provides for His flock.

Psalm 23:5

You prepare a table before me
    in the presence of my enemies.
You anoint my head with oil;
    my cup overflows.

7. *You prepare a table before me in the presence of my enemies (23:5).* Why does the promise of vindication help us endure the injustices of life? How can we bring these things to God in prayer without "cursing our enemies"?

_____

_____

58

_____

_____

_____

_____

8. *My cup overflows (23:5)*. What is life like when it seems as though it just can't contain all the blessings of God? How does the memory of times like these, or the prospect of them, help us endure leaner times?

_____

_____

_____

_____

_____

9. What could God change in your life right now to make everything perfect?

_____

_____

_____

_____

_____

Optional Application: Make believe you are preparing a table at which your enemies will dine. What will you serve? What will your choices say about how far along you are in the forgiveness process?

For Further Study: Read about the anointing of David in 1 Samuel 16: "Samuel took the horn of oil and anointed [David] in the presence of his brothers, and from that day on the Spirit of the Lord came powerfully upon David. Samuel then went to Ramah" (verse 13). What might have reminded David about this time as he wrote Psalm 23?

In the presence of my enemies. Many view this phrase as a picture of eventual reconciliation with our enemies, to the point that we will be able to sit down and share a meal with them. More than likely, this refers to the victorious kings' practice of chaining conquered kings and princes to the pillars in a banquet hall, forcing them to watch the celebration of their defeat. The enemy kings that David conquered were ruthless and merciless men. To celebrate in this manner would have been considered an expression of God's vindication (for which David and others ask repeatedly throughout the Psalms).

For Thought and Discussion: How have you seen the goodness and love of God evident every day of your life, even the bad ones? Why is it sometimes easier to see the influence of God in hindsight than in the middle of a difficult time?

Psalm 23:6

Surely your goodness and love will follow me
    all the days of my life,
and I will dwell in the house of the LORD
    forever.

10. *Surely your goodness and love will follow me (23:6).* How long does it usually take for the blessing of God (for example, the good in a seemingly bad situation) to catch up with you after a difficult experience?

_____

_____

_____

11. *I will dwell in the house of the LORD (23:6).* In what sense do we dwell in God's house now, today? What does the word *dwelling* mean to you?

_____

_____

_____

12. What is it about connecting with God that brings about a sense of renewal and restoration?

_____

_____

_____

_____

Dwelling. To be given privileges in the king's "house" was considered a great honor. This honor was given to Mephibosheth, the crippled son of Jonathan, because of David's promise to Jonathan, his best friend. Mephibosheth was given a place at the king's table, and all of his grandfather Saul's lands were restored to him. Perhaps David had this mercy in mind he wrote about dwelling in the Lord's house.

For the group

Warm-up. Psalm 23 is often read at funerals. Although memorial services are typically sad experiences, some of them can be celebratory events of a life well lived and honoring to God. Ask group members if any of them have attended such a funeral and why it was special. What about the sentiments in Psalm 23 ministered to the loved ones at that funeral?

Questions. Many of today's questions focus on the renewing aspect of prayer. Often when we talk with God, a sense of peace and comfort comes upon us that is difficult to explain. It is often this need for renewal and rest that drives us to prayer as we try to sustain ourselves through the weary battles of life. Some of the questions in this lesson talk about the soothing, reenergizing nature of God's Spirit. Help the group see that prayer can revive their spirits just as a hot tub can refresh a body.

Prayer. During group prayer, focus on the specific ways in which God has renewed your soul and spirit through prayer. Give thanks for the ways in which the people in your class have brought joy and a sense of renewal to you. It's important to model the types of prayers you're discussing.

Optional Application: Describe your ideal "room" in the house of the LORD. What will it include? What do these things you listed reflect about the healthy aspects of your spiritual walk?

For Further Study: Fast-forward to Jesus' promise to His disciples: "My Father's house has many rooms; if that were not so, would I have told you that I am going there to prepare a place for you?" (John 14:2). Why do you think Jesus describes our reward as a "house"? In what ways will we finally feel "home" when we get to heaven? Explain.

PRAYER: LOOKING TO THE PAST, PLANNING FOR THE FUTURE

We have heard with our ears, O God; our
ancestors have told us what you did in their
days, in days long ago. (Psalm 44:1)

Lesson Objective: That participants will see that
our confidence in the future comes from looking to
what God has done for us in the past.

Desired Action: That participants will remind
themselves of God's faithfulness when they are fac-
ing future challenges.

Psalms for This Lesson: 44, 78, 85, 87, 90, 95, 99,
106, 114, 126, 132, 135

We find that many psalms are steeped with historical references, specifically of times in the Israelites'
past in which they experienced the deliverance of
God. By looking to the past, the psalmists gained
confidence for the future. Certainly we can follow this example in our prayers. So much of the
Christian faith centers upon "remembrance." In the
same way, as we look to the ways in our individual
histories that God has delivered us, we can look to
the future confident that God is still going to act
and intervene on our behalf.

For Thought and Discussion: How have you seen God at work in the generations that preceded you? How have you been impacted spiritually by your ancestors?

Optional Application: Describe a typical day as if it represented an entire lifetime (birth is waking up, death is falling asleep at the end of the day). What happens in between? How do these events represent different aspects of your life? How does this activity help you understand how God can view a thousand years, or the seventy- or eighty-some years of a typical lifetime, as if they were a day?

Psalm 90:1-6

A prayer of Moses the man of God.

Lord, you have been our dwelling place
   throughout all generations.
Before the mountains were born
   or you brought forth the whole world,
   from everlasting to everlasting you are God.

You turn people back to dust,
   saying, "Return to dust, you mortals."
A thousand years in your sight
   are like a day that has just gone by,
   or like a watch in the night.
Yet you sweep people away in the sleep of death—
   they are like the new grass of the morning:
In the morning it springs up new,
   but by evening it is dry and withered.

1. *From everlasting to everlasting you are God (90:2).* Why is it helpful to see our lives in the context of cosmic history?

   Just a short stint in the big picture

2. *A thousand years in your sight are like a day that has just gone by (90:4).* How can God see our lives, from beginning to end, in a matter of moments? How does this truth put things in perspective for us in regard to our prayers?

   God is omnipotent. When we are going thru painful period, seems like long time. Earthly life is small piece.

3. What is comforting about the relative shortness of life in God's eyes? How does it help us to understand His unwavering grasp on the smallest details of our lives?

   Spurgeon.org
   Psalm 31

64

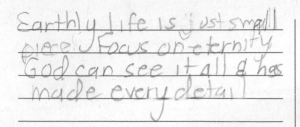

Earthly life is just small piece. Focus on eternity. God can see it all & has made every detail.

Return to dust. "Ashes to ashes, dust to dust." This old English burial rite comes from Genesis 3:19:

> By the sweat of your brow
>   you will eat your food
> until you return to the ground,
>   since from it you were taken;
> for dust you are
>   and to dust you will return.

The psalmist is simply acknowledging that the statement of God to Adam still holds true: We will return to the dust, utterly dependent on the sovereignty of God to give us our lives back.

Psalm 90:7-9

> We are consumed by your anger
>   and terrified by your indignation.
> You have set our iniquities before you,
>   our secret sins in the light of your presence.
> All our days pass away under your wrath;
>   we finish our years with a moan.

4. _We are consumed by your anger and terrified by your indignation (90:7)._ Under what circumstances would the LORD be angry with Christians? What can we learn from Christ's admonitions to the seven churches in Revelation in this regard (Revelation 1–3)?

Leaving first love. Need to repent or do work's. Idols and fornication

For Further Study: Peter was probably referring to Psalm 90 when he wrote, "Do not forget this one thing, dear friends: With the Lord a day is like a thousand years, and a thousand years are like a day" (2 Peter 3:8). Pick any thousand-year period in history (from the time of Abraham to King Solomon, or Moses to Malachi, or the time between Rome's becoming a Republic and Martin Luther's nailing the ninety-five theses to the Wittenburg Door). Try to imagine that God sees the events of these thousand-year periods unfolding in the span of twenty-four hours. Staggering, isn't it?

For Thought and Discussion: Have you ever felt terrified by God? Isaiah and Daniel felt terror in the presence of God; what can we learn from the example of these godly men?

John 1:9
Hebrew 4:

5. *You have set our iniquities before you, our secret sins in the light of your presence (90:8).* How are your prayers affected by the fact that we can hide nothing from God? Why is it better to just acknowledge what God knows already?

Need to confess and repent. God knows all, better to seek God and be honest.

6. How can we derive comfort and confidence from the ways God has dealt with our sins and disciplined us in the past?

Son died on cross to save us.

The revealing light of God's presence.
Throughout the Scriptures, it is the "light of God's presence" that reveals everything the impenitent heart wants to keep hidden. He reveals the deep things of darkness and brings deep shadows into the light (see Job 12:22). Everyone who does evil hates the light and will not come into the light for fear that his deeds will be exposed (see John 3:20). Nothing causes evil men to disappear more quickly than to shine the light on their wicked deeds.

Psalm 90:10-12

Our days may come to seventy years,
  or eighty, if our strength endures;
yet the best of them are but trouble and sorrow,
  for they quickly pass, and we fly away.

If only we knew the power of your anger!
　　Your wrath is as great as the fear that is your due.
　Teach us to number our days,
　　that we may gain a heart of wisdom.

7. *Our days may come to seventy years, or eighty, if our strength endures (90:10).* Based on your family history, how many years do you think you have left?

Mom - 94 - 30 to 40

_____

_____

_____

8. *Teach us to number our days, that we may gain a heart of wisdom (90:12).* What is it about knowing that our time is limited that causes us to value that time more deeply? Why is it so easy to take our time for granted?

− _Treat every moment as precious - as its your last_
− _Think you have unlimited time, put off doing things_

9. Ten years from now, what might you wish you would have done for the kingdom? What can you start doing this week to prevent that particular regret?

− _Volunteered more time_
− _Give more_
− _Share Jesus_
− _Volunteer, give, share_

For Thought and Discussion: If you could plan for your last day on earth, one in which you were perfectly healthy in all respects and had every financial resource at your disposal, how would you spend that day?

Optional Application: Lay out five to ten index cards on a table. Take one card for each decade of future life you think (and hope) God will give you. On each card, write down three things you would like to see happen in that specific decade.

For Further Study: Read Genesis 5 and note the significantly long life spans of the men listed. What happened between that time and the time of David, when people were living seventy to eighty years on average?

Numbering our days. Jesus reflected the sentiment of "numbering our days" when He said, "Can any one of you by worrying add a single hour to your life?" (Matthew 6:27). The essence of this biblical principle is that God has determined, in

His sovereignty, exactly how long each person is going to live. Because there's nothing we can do to change that decision, we are to value and tap into every minute of life God has given us.

Psalm 90:13-17

Relent, Lord! How long will it be?
 Have compassion on your servants.
Satisfy us in the morning with your unfailing love,
 that we may sing for joy and be glad all our days.
Make us glad for as many days as you have afflicted us,
 for as many years as we have seen trouble.
May your deeds be shown to your servants,
 your splendor to their children.

May the favor of the Lord our God rest on us;
 establish the work of our hands for us—
 yes, establish the work of our hands.

10. *Make us glad for as many days as you have afflicted us, for as many years as we have seen trouble (90:15).* What is it about the promise of God's restoration that helps us deal with life's losses? Why should we grieve those losses, especially in prayer, even though one day God will "restore to you the years that the locust hath eaten" (Joel 2:25, KJV)?

— You know light at end of tunnel, happier days.
— Need to be honest with your feelings, express emotion

11. *May the favor of the Lord our God rest on us; establish the work of our hands for us (90:17).* Why is it important to pronounce blessings like this, in prayer, for what we hope will happen in the future? How will such a blessing affect our thinking when those blessings do come?

Need God's hands and his will for us

Hands - what we offer to God

_____

_____

_____

_____

_____

12. What are your hopes for future generations, should the Lord tarry, based on how God has blessed you and your generation?

Peace, freedom to worship God blesses nation

_____

_____

_____

Hands. There are more than five hundred references to hands in the Bible. Quite often in these references, the hands of believers are used metaphorically to describe what we offer to God. We offer hard work to God with our hands (see 1 Corinthians 4:12); we lift up holy hands in praise to God (see 1 Timothy 2:8); we lay hands on others for healing and to affirm their gifts (see Hebrews 6:2). Our hands are one of the primary means by which we communicate the grace of God to others and the means by which we bear fruit for the kingdom.

For the group

Warm-up. When David was asked where he got the courage to fight Goliath, he replied, "'The LORD who rescued me from the paw of the lion and the paw of the bear will rescue me from the hand of this Philistine.' Saul said to David, 'Go, and the LORD be with you.'" (1 Samuel 17:37). Today's lesson encourages people to remember the ways God has delivered them in the past in order to find faith and hope for the challenges ahead. Ask for volunteers to talk about the ways God has delivered them in the past. These

Optional Application: Write out a blessing for a family member. Plan on delivering that blessing this week, either in writing or, preferably, in person. Warning: This blessing could change that person's outlook on life, for the rest of his or her life.

For Further Study: Psalm 90 asks for God's blessing on the work of his servants. This idea is reflected in a later psalm: "Unless the LORD builds the house, the builders labor in vain" (Psalm 127:1). What other projects in the Bible failed because God's hand was not in the work (for example, the Tower of Babel)? What mistakes did the people make with these doomed projects?

stories will serve as the basis for today's prayer: thanking God for past rescues as we look to Him to help us, once again, in the imminent battles.

Questions. This lesson's questions focus on looking at life "all at once"—in many ways, from God's perspective. The questions call for lots of reflecting. Again, the goal is to build group members' confidence that God knows everything about them, from beginning to end. And God knows the multiple ways in which He has delivered them and will in the future. Encourage group members to increase their faith by looking back on the faithfulness of God throughout their entire lives.

Prayer. Be ready to thank God in prayer for the things He has done throughout your life. Model the type of prayer that recalls God's faithfulness in the past in order to gain confidence for the future. By the end of your prayer time, hopefully you and the group members will think, *Wow, there's nothing that my God cannot do!*

PRAYER AND THE APPARENT SILENCE OF GOD

Why, Lord, do you stand far off? Why do you hide
yourself in times of trouble? (Psalm 10:1)

Lesson Objective: That participants will not think it
strange that sometimes God appears to be silent and
not answering our prayers.

Desired Action: That participants will endure their
own "dark nights of the soul" with patience and
perseverance. What do we do when it does not seem
that God is responding to us, much less listening to
anything we have to say?

Psalms for This Lesson: 6, 10, 13, 22, 42, 50, 77

Throughout the history of the people of God, deeply
devoted followers have found themselves in what has
been called "the dark night of the soul," character-
ized by an increased awareness of personal sin and
the seeming inability to connect with God through
prayer or any other form of worship. In fact, the
desire to do so decreases with every failed attempt.
We see a lot of this in the Psalms, where the writer
wants to hear from God but experiences nothing but
silence. The contemporary believer should expect
nothing less. But it is in the expectation that the
experience becomes less surprising. Usually, it is
simply a matter of time before the fog lifts and our
prayers, once again, drift heavenward. But in the
meantime, God has much to teach us during these

dark periods, even thought it seems we seldom, if ever, hear from Him directly.

Psalm 10:1-2,17-18

Why, LORD, do you stand far off?
  Why do you hide yourself in times of trouble?
In his arrogance the wicked man hunts down the weak,
  who are caught in the schemes he devises. . . .
You, LORD, hear the desire of the afflicted;
  you encourage them, and you listen to their cry,
defending the fatherless and the oppressed,
  so that mere earthly mortals
  will never again strike terror.

1. *Why, LORD, do you stand far off? (10:1).* Why does the apparent silence of God seem so puzzling to us? When we pray and pray but heaven seems closed, how are we to understand God's promise to hear our prayers?

_____

_____

_____

_____

2. *You, LORD, hear the desire of the afflicted (10:17).* What are your top three desires during extremely difficult circumstances, when life seems to be nothing but one disabling event after another?

_____

_____

_____

_____

3. Why do we especially need to hear from God when our difficulties are caused by the deliberate malice of others?

_____

_____

_____

_____

Hunting. Hunting for game is mentioned frequently in the Bible. Of course, a degree of deception is involved on the part of the hunter in order to lure the game in and get it to relax and not attempt to take flight until it's too late. Surely the psalmist has this in mind when he writes about the wicked man who hunts down the weak. The predator is always looking for the vulnerabilities of his target.

Psalm 13:1-6

For the director of music. A psalm of David.

> How long, Lord? Will you forget me forever?
>   How long will you hide your face from me?
> How long must I wrestle with my thoughts
>   and day after day have sorrow in my heart?
>   How long will my enemy triumph over me?
>
> Look on me and answer, Lord my God.
>   Give light to my eyes, or I will sleep in death,
> and my enemy will say, "I have overcome him,"
>   and my foes will rejoice when I fall.
> But I trust in your unfailing love;
>   my heart rejoices in your salvation.
> I will sing the Lord's praise,
>   for he has been good to me.

4. *How long must I wrestle with my thoughts (13:2)?* When your thoughts get into a wrestling match, which ones usually win? Why does the mind's tumble of racing thoughts seem to go on forever? What can you do to stop them?

_____

_____

_____

_____

Optional Application: Look outside and find the farthest point you can see. What types of circumstances in life make you feel as though God is this far from you?

For Further Study: Read about Saul's pursuit of David, an example of a wicked man hunting down the weak (see 1 Samuel 26). How did God eventually make it so that Saul could "never again strike terror" (Psalm 10:18)?

For Thought and Discussion: When a person is struggling through a time of spiritual darkness, it's hard to find any hope. If you know someone like this, offer to "hope for" the person as he or she endures this difficult time. And if you're going through such a time yourself, find a mature believer who will do this for you.

Optional Application: Sing a simple hymn of praise to God no matter how you might be feeling at the moment.

For Further Study: Read through the book of Lamentations. How did Jeremiah express his hope in God even during the forced exile of his people (which he had warned them over and over was going to happen)?

5. *I trust in your unfailing love (13:5).* Why is it better to trust in something that does not change, such as God's love, than in our feelings about how much God may or may not love us?

_____

_____

_____

_____

6. *I will sing the Lord's praise, for he has been good to me (13:6).* Why do people who are down often think they will never feel again better? Why is it important for them to believe that one day they will sing again?

_____

_____

_____

_____

How long? In this two-worded question, the psalmist captures the human agony of waiting for a trial to be over or for an injustice to be righted. In fact, the question is asked four times in Psalm 13. But even so, the psalmist is assured that God will act in His perfect timing. This question is even asked by the glorified souls of martyrs under the heavenly altar:

When he opened the fifth seal, I saw under the altar the souls of those who had been slain because of the word of God and the testimony they had maintained. They called out in a loud voice, "How long, Sovereign Lord, holy and true, until you judge the inhabitants of the earth and avenge our blood?" Then each of them was

74

given a white robe, and they were told to wait a little longer, until the full number of their fellow servants, their brothers and sisters, were killed just as they had been." (Revelation 6:9-11)

Psalm 22:1-2

For the director of music. To the tune of "The Doe of the Morning." A psalm of David.

My God, my God, why have you forsaken me?
Why are you so far from saving me,
so far from my cries of anguish?
My God, I cry out by day, but you do not answer,
by night, but I find no rest.

7. *My God, my God, why have you forsaken me? (22:1).* How is Christ our supreme example when it comes to praying fervently even when it seems God is not listening?

_____

_____

_____

_____

_____

_____

8. *My God, I cry out by day, but you do not answer (22:2).* Why is it important to express our frustration with God when He doesn't seem to be answering? Do you think this angers Him? Explain.

_____

_____

_____

_____

_____

For Thought and Discussion: If Christ can feel forsaken by God, how much more so should we expect to feel forsaken at some point in our lives? Jesus told us that the servant will never be greater than the master. If the master has experienced a trial, so will the disciple.

75

Optional Application: Take a moment to meditate on these words of Christ on the cross. What have you gone through that would help you empathize with His feeling forsaken? Express that empathy to Him in prayer.

For Further Study: Read through the passion narrative in the gospel of John (19:18-21). What combination of events during this time period would have led up to Jesus' cry, "My God, my God, why have you forsaken me?" (Matthew 27:46).

For Thought and Discussion: The judgment of God should be a sobering thing for the people of God. He who understands every motive of the heart will one day hold each of us accountable for our deeds and words. Even so, God still entrusts us with responsibilities for the kingdom. What does it mean to be trusted by someone from whom we can hide nothing?

9. Read all of Psalm 22. Christ had the entire psalm in mind on the cross when He quoted the first verse. From what we read in this psalm, what can we learn about Christ's mindset during this time of deep crisis?

_____

_____

_____

_____

_____

A messianic lament. Although Jesus quotes only part of Psalm 22 aloud on the cross, so much of it reflects His experience: "All who see me mock me; they hurl insults, shaking their heads. 'He trusts in the LORD, 'they say,' let the LORD rescue him. Let him deliver him, since he delights in him.'" (verses 7-8); "All my bones are on display; people stare and gloat over me. They divide my clothes among them and cast lots for my garment" (verses 17-18). But Christ was thinking not only about the lamenting part of this psalm but also about its second half, which rejoices in God's sovereignty.

Psalm 50:3-5

A psalm of Asaph.

Our God comes
    and will not be silent;
a fire devours before him,
    and around him a tempest rages.
He summons the heavens above,
    and the earth, that he may judge his people:
"Gather to me this consecrated people,
    who made a covenant with me by sacrifice."

10. *Our God comes and will not be silent (50:3).* What is it about the apparent silence of God that is just that—apparent? What do you think God is trying to do for us when He appears to be nonresponsive?

_____

_____

_____

_____

_____

11. *"Gather to me this consecrated people, who made a covenant with me by sacrifice" (50:5).* What is the promise of God here, especially during times when our prayers seem to be bouncing off the ceiling?

_____

_____

_____

_____

12. Sometimes extended periods of God's silence end in a firestorm of supernatural activity in our lives. How can we best prepare for this as we wait for God to move?

_____

_____

_____

_____

Optional Application: Draw a picture of the most spectacular experience of God that you've ever had in your life. Maybe it was so intense that all you can do is draw a symbol of what happened. What is it about this experience that has set it apart from all others in your mind?

For Further Study: Read about the judgment of Christ followers in 1 Corinthians 3:10-15. How can the quality of our works be judged if we're saved by grace? What phrase in this passage tells us that this particular judgment has nothing to do with salvation?

Covenant. The Hebrew word for *covenant*, at its root, means "to cut." Perhaps this is why, in today's terms, a covenant is an agreement between parties to "cut a deal." Covenants are mentioned more than three hundred times in the Scriptures, so it's easy to speculate about their importance. Covenants spell out expectations for each party entering into an agreement. If one party does not fulfill his or her obligations of the covenant, the agreement is nullified. As we see in Psalm 50, God always keeps His part of the covenants He's agreed to.

77

For the group

Warm-up. Ask for volunteers to talk about a time in their lives when it seemed God was far off even though they weren't caught up in any particular sin and even their church lives and ministries were thriving. You might be surprised to hear how common these periods of spiritual dryness are. But God wants us to keep praying, even when it seems no one is listening.

Questions. Many of the questions in this lesson deal with a type of raw candor with God that some group members may find disrespectful or irreverent. Assure them that this is the example set for us by the psalmists. There's nothing disrespectful about telling God how frustrated or confused we are. Again, the best thing we can do in prayer is to acknowledge what is plainly seen by God. So to express happy, lofty expressions of praise when our hearts are actually heavy with pain and injustice can be more disrespectful to God than simply expressing what is true.

Prayer. Because this lesson is about the silence of God, end the lesson with silent prayer. Remind group members that no one knows the silent thoughts of a person except God and that individual. It's because of this truth that silent prayer can become a type of sanctuary for a very private conversation between a human being and his or her Maker.

PRAYER AND WAITING ON THE LORD

Wait for the LORD; be strong and take heart and
wait for the LORD. (Psalm 27:14)

Lesson Objective: That participants will understand
that they must submit themselves to God's timing
in regard to their prayerful requests.

Desired Action: That participants will persist in
their prayers as they wait to hear from God.

Psalms for This Lesson: 27, 33, 37, 40, 130

It's common to hear statistics about how much of our
life is consumed by waiting: waiting at the grocery
store, or the bank, or for a seat in a restaurant, or for
the phone to ring. Waiting on the Lord, however, is
never a waste of time. It is one of the most difficult,
but ultimately satisfying, spiritual disciplines. If we
are responsible believers, we will know what actions
we should take in response to a challenge or crisis and
then actually take those steps. But once we reach the
point where we've accomplished everything we legiti-
mately can, there's nothing left to do but wait on the
Lord. He alone knows the "big picture" of what's going
on, and so He understands what else needs to happen,
what other roles need to be played out, in order for our
desired outcomes to happen. And so we spend this
time trusting in God's sovereignty and, more times
than not, ending up utterly surprised at what God was
doing while we were waiting.

Psalm 27:13-14

Of David.

> I remain confident of this:
> > I will see the goodness of the LORD
> > in the land of the living.
>
> Wait for the LORD;
> > be strong and take heart
> > and wait for the LORD.

1. *I remain confident of this: I will see the goodness of the LORD (27:13).* What often happens to your confidence levels when there's nothing more you can do and we must wait on the LORD?

   - Goes down, waiting a long time
   - Go up, nothing you can do in God's hand - confiden in him

2. *Wait for the LORD; be strong and take heart (27:14).* How do you determine when you've done all you can do and a situation is entirely in God's hands? From what can you draw strength when there's nothing more to do but wait?

   - When you don't know what to do next
   - faith in God, perfect timing, works all things for good

3. Is waiting on God necessarily a passive thing, where we're doing nothing? What does God expect us to do while we wait for His perfect timing?

   Pray, praise

_____

_____

Land of the living. The psalmist uses this phrase in contrast to the "land of the dead," or "Sheol," where the dead go, in Jewish thought, to await judgment. The psalmist's point is that he is confident God is going to act decisively in this age and in the age to come.

Psalm 40:1-3

For the director of music. Of David. A psalm.

> I waited patiently for the LORD;
>   he turned to me and heard my cry.
> He lifted me out of the slimy pit,
>   out of the mud and mire;
> he set my feet on a rock
>   and gave me a firm place to stand.
> He put a new song in my mouth,
>   a hymn of praise to our God.
> Many will see and fear the LORD
>   and put their trust in him.

4. *I waited patiently for the LORD (40:1).* Why is waiting on God often challenging to our patience? What can impatience during this time tempt us to do?

- Yes, answer does not come fast enough
- Take it into your own hands

_____

5. *He put a new song in my mouth (40:3).* What kinds of things can you learn only during times of trouble while waiting for God's deliverance? What is so "new" about this new song?

Patience, perseverance

For Thought and Discussion: What does the recovery process after a crisis typically look like for you? Think back on a difficult time in which you faced a health, financial, or relational crisis — one that eventually resolved well. Did you feel your spirit lifting as you began to realize that a workable solution was in sight? Are you able now to wholly attribute that deliverance to God?

Optional Application: Make a list of the prayers you're waiting for God to answer. Go through your list and ask Him, "How are we doing on this request, Lord? Just checking in."

For Further Study: Read about Jeremiah's imprisonment and rescue in Jeremiah 38, when he was thrown into a slimy, muddy cistern. Jeremiah would have known Psalm 40; how do you think it might have helped him during this difficult and extremely unjust time?

_____

_____

_____

_____

6. *Many will see and fear the LORD and put their trust in him (40:3).* Why does the power of God seem more obvious after a relatively long period of waiting for Him to act? Why should this encourage us all the more to hang in there while we're waiting on God's timing?

_____

_____

_____

_____

_____

He turned to me. Are there times when God has His back to us, times when He doesn't know what's going on until He turns around? No, the psalmist is using an *anthropomorphism* here; he is attributing typically human characteristics to God so that we can better understand and interpret our experience of Him. God is omniscient; He knows everything that's going on at every moment of time. But waiting for God can seem as though we're waiting to get His attention. In actuality, He is fully aware of our situation and of our requests for deliverance.

Psalm 37:3-7

Trust in the LORD and do good;
    dwell in the land and enjoy safe pasture.
Take delight in the LORD,
    and he will give you the desires of your heart.

Commit your way to the LORD;
    trust in him and he will do this:
He will make your righteous reward shine like the dawn,
    your vindication like the noonday sun.

Be still before the LORD
    and wait patiently for him;
do not fret when people succeed in their ways,
    when they carry out their wicked schemes.

God giver want— seed

7. *Take delight in the LORD, and he will give you the desires of your heart (37:4).* Does this promise mean that God gives us what we want, or does He plant the actual desires within our hearts? In either case, what's the prerequisite for this happening?

In touch with God,
Communicate with him

For Thought and Discussion: How do your desires shape the plans of your life? What is your life like today because of the plans you made ten, twenty, perhaps even thirty years ago?

Phillipians 4:8

8. *Commit your way to the LORD (37:5).* Why it is important to lay out all our plans in front of God before we move forward? What often happens to our plans that don't have His blessing?

9. *Be still before the LORD and wait patiently for him (37:7).* Why do a lot of people get restless while waiting for God to intervene? What is it about deliberate stillness in the Lord that clarifies our thinking?

Optional Application: Make out your plans for next Thursday, listing everything you're pretty sure is going to happen. Commit that day to God by bringing your plans to Him first.

For Further Study: Look up some of the villains of the Bible (for example, Cain, Genesis 4; King Manasseh, 2 Chronicles 33; or Haman, Esther 3–7). and calculate how long they remained in power and caused grief for so many people. Be sure to find out how their stories ended. If God would allow these people to do their evil works for forty or fifty years, what should that tell us about His willingness to allow some people today to carry out their "wicked schemes" (Psalm 37:7)?

For Thought and Discussion: What is the relationship between *hope, trust,* and *love* in Psalm 33? How do you see each of these feeding the other two in your life?

Safe pasture. Again the psalmist appeals to shepherding imagery to help us understand God's nurturing and protective nature. A safe pasture isn't necessarily one that's predator-free, but the rich meadow is protected by a shepherd who has a vested interest in each one of his sheep (unlike a hired hand who bolts at the first sign of danger).

Psalm 33:20-22

We wait in hope for the LORD;
    he is our help and our shield.
In him our hearts rejoice,
    for we trust in his holy name.
May your unfailing love be with us, LORD,
    even as we put our hope in you.

10. *We wait in hope for the LORD (33:20).* What difference does hope make when we're waiting? What is it like for someone who waits in despair?

= See positive result
— Despair - negative result

11. *May your unfailing love be with us, LORD (33:22).* What is it about God's love that we can count on, no matter how we're feeling?

84

Shield. At the time the psalm was written, there were basically two types of shields in use. The first, the *tsinnah*, was a large shield often worn by well-equipped infantry. This shield could be as big as a door and was intended to protect the entire soldier. The *maghen* was much smaller, often round in shape. Its primary use was in hand-to-hand combat, whereas the larger *tsinnah* was meant to make the soldier less vulnerable in the open field. One can see where the psalmist might have had either type in mind when using the shield as a metaphor for God's protective power.

For the group

Warm-up. Ask for volunteers to talk about the different things they wait for in life. Perhaps you can even look up some interesting waiting statistics (for example, "We spend a total of seven months of our lives waiting in grocery lines, even if we choose the *Ten Items or Less* lanes"). This lesson intends to contrast these times of involuntary waiting with the process of waiting on the Lord. Being patient with God's timing is an important discipline in our spiritual growth to maturity. Remind your group that God is going to give them plenty of opportunities to exercise this discipline!

Questions. The questions in this lesson are intended to encourage submission to the sovereignty of God. Waiting on the Lord to act—and not taking presumptuous actions to speed things along—is the focus of the psalms you'll study in this lesson. The questions will also focus on what to do while we're waiting. Waiting on God is not a passive activity; it's an act of submission in which we bow to God's will and perfect timing and move on with the other tasks He has given us to do.

Prayer. Let the prayer time convey an attitude of humble submission to the will and the timing of God. Model for the group what it means to concede that God's timing is perfect and how foolish it would be to try to hasten the fulfillment of any of God's promises. Look at what happened to Abraham when he tried to circumvent God's plans: Ishmael was the

Optional Application: Find a small box and call it your hope chest. What kinds of things would you put in it (if they'd fit)? What sorts of things are you hoping and waiting for?

For Further Study: Do a Bible keyword study on the word *shield*. (There are nearly a hundred references.) Note the times shield is used to describe a literal defensive weapon and when it's used as a metaphor for God's protection. How do all of the literal references support the analogies?

85

father of some of the Jews' fiercest enemies today, and all because Abraham wouldn't wait on the Lord (see Genesis 16–17). Let us learn from his impatience and simply wait on God to act only in His perfect timing.

PRAYERS OF REWARD AND THANKSGIVING

We praise you, God, we praise you,
for your Name is near; people tell
of your wonderful deeds. (Psalm 75:1)

Lesson Objective: That participants will believe that God rewards their prayers with specific answers and action and that their natural response to God's active involvement should be one of deep gratitude.

Desired Action: That participants will be aware of the specific ways in which God has answered their prayers and that they will constantly offer up thanks for the multitude of things He does for them, especially for how much He loves and cares for them.

Psalms for This Lesson: 37, 41, 45, 58, 72, 75, 84, 100, 105, 107, 112, 128, 133, 144, 145

The psalms of reward and thanksgiving focus on the blessings of God and our response of appreciation for those gifts. We need look no further than ourselves to know how good it feels to be the recipient of someone's genuine gratitude. In fact, gratitude sometimes compels us to want to continue helping or rewarding that thankful person. God is no different. He deeply desires for us to acknowledge with words of thanksgiving from the heart the abundance of blessings He has poured out on us. For this reason, the psalmists are constantly expressing awe and thanks for the ways God consistently blesses His servants.

For Thought and Discussion: Why does the psalmist tell us to make our relationship with God our first priority (for example, "trust in the LORD . . . take delight in the LORD")? Do you think God gives us the desire to do what He wants us to do?

Psalm 37:3-5

Trust in the LORD and do good;
dwell in the land and enjoy safe pasture.
Take delight in the LORD,
and he will give you the desires of your heart.

Commit your way to the LORD;
trust in him and he will do this.

1. *Trust in the LORD and do good (37:1).* How does this command show us the relationship between faith and works? According to this verse, how will a person who does good be rewarded?

   — First, you have to have faith
   Then do good works
   — Safe pasture, desire of
   your heart

2. What are the relational conditions of reward here? Why are they reasonable?

   Trust and take delight

3. What are some ways we can express our trust and delight in the Lord through prayer?

Safe pasture. There is an amazing amount of rocks in the Holy Land. They are strewn all over the place. You need not take a step to find a rock or boulder; just reach down and you're likely to find all the rocks you need. Even in the pastures of ancient Israel, the land is full of rocks and boulders behind which enemies could hide: wolves, bears, lions, and other thieves (human and animal). The idea of "safe pasture" could be guaranteed only by a shepherd who was totally committed to the well-being of the flock, not a day laborer who would run at the first sign of danger. This is the confidence we can have in our Shepherd, the Lord Jesus Christ.

Optional Application: List the top ten desires of your heart. Rank them in their order of importance to you. Ask yourself, *Why has God given me this desire? What will He expect of me as He fulfills it?*

Psalm 58:11

For Further Study: Read Psalm 145. Compare the conditions of fulfilled desires in this psalm with the passage we just studied.

Then people will say,
"Surely the righteous still are rewarded;
surely there is a God who judges the earth."

4. *"Surely there is a God who judges the earth" (58:11)*. What would the world be like if God were to never hold people accountable for their actions? If you thought that you'd never stand before God, how would you be different?

People would do whatever
they desire-selfish,
lawless, cruel

For Thought and Discussion: Why do you think the Scriptures speak so often of reward? Is it wrong for the Christian to be motivated by reward?

5. When we start recalling our blessings in prayer, what is our natural response to God?

Thanksgiving

6. Why do we feel compelled to thank a person when he or she gives us a gift or does something for us? What are some reasons other than it being the polite thing to do?

Optional Application: Once a day for the next week, do something out of the ordinary for someone and gauge his or her response. Open a door, compliment an outfit, notice well-behaved kids. If the person thanks you, take note of how he or she expresses gratitude. If the person doesn't thank you, notice how you feel.

For Further Study: Read all of Psalm 58. Why are the righteous rewarded in this psalm? How does this prayer reflect the biblical adage "Vengeance is mine; I will repay, saith the Lord" (Romans 12:19, KJV)? Are these types of prayers appropriate for us today?

For Thought and Discussion: What is it about being grateful that prevents us from taking certain things for granted? Why is it important to have someone to thank (instead of just "feeling" grateful)?

Like the venom of a snake. The psalmist compares the venom of the wicked with that of a cobra. In ancient times, the spitting cobra could spray its venom about eight feet. It aimed for the eyes, causing temporary blindness and excruciating pain. The venom of cobras is a neurotoxin that acts quickly and powerfully on the nervous system. No wonder the psalmist gives thanks for God's deliverance from the venom of his enemies.

Psalm 100:1-5

A psalm. For giving thanks.

> Shout for joy to the LORD, all the earth.
> Worship the LORD with gladness;
> come before him with joyful songs.
> Know that the LORD is God.
> It is he who made us, and we are his;
> we are his people, the sheep of his pasture.
>
> Enter his gates with thanksgiving
> and his courts with praise;
> give thanks to him and praise his name.
> For the LORD is good and his love endures forever;
> his faithfulness continues through all generations.

7. *Worship the LORD with gladness (100:2).* Why are worship and thanksgiving so intrinsically linked? Why does one often result in the other?

8. *Singing and shouting.* Why do we sometimes want to publicly express our thanks for the things people have done for us? Why does it make it extra special to be thanked in this way? Why is it appropriate to publicly thank God for the things He has done?

_____

_____

_____

_____

_____

_____

_____

9. What makes privately expressed thanks special? When we express our thanks privately to God in prayer, what are we communicating to Him about our relationship with Him?

_____

_____

_____

_____

_____

_____

Optional Application: See if your church will allow you to publish a public thank-you in the bulletin for someone's faithful, behind-the-scenes work. Consider taking out a classified ad in the local newspaper expressing thanks for someone's special gift to you.

For Further Study: Scan Psalms 41, 45, 72, 75, 84, 105, 107, 112, 128, 133, 144, and 145. Note all the different ways the psalmists express thanks to God. Also note the things for which they are grateful.

His gates. Ancient cities were built like fortresses, with walls reaching twenty to fifty feet in height and fortified gates for entrances. Jerusalem alone had sixteen such gates. Quite often when a king returned from a successful campaign, the pageantry of his entrance through a city's main gate was quite extravagant. David was known to "enter the gates" (see Psalm 100:4) of the city with songs of praise and thanksgiving for what God had just successfully accomplished through him (for example, see 2 Samuel 6:5).

For Thought and Discussion: Why is it that when someone says, "Hey, thanks for everything," the expression feels a little empty? Why is it that we'd usually prefer that people be specific about what they appreciate?

Optional Application: List some of the wonderful deeds God has accomplished on your behalf just this week. As you thank Him in prayer, be specific about how you appreciate each thing.

For Further Study: Read the story of the woman at the well in John 4. How do the actions of God in Psalm 107 compare with what Jesus promised to the woman who was seeking to satisfy her thirst?

Psalm 107:8-9

Let them give thanks to the LORD for his unfailing love
  and his wonderful deeds for mankind,
for he satisfies the thirsty
  and fills the hungry with good things.

10. *Give thanks . . . for his unfailing love, and his wonderful deeds for mankind (107:8).* Why do you think the psalmist gets very specific in his expression of thanks here?

_____

_____

_____

_____

11. *He satisfies the thirsty and fills the hungry with good things (107:9).* Do you think the psalmist is being literal or figurative here? Or both? How does this expression compare with what Jesus promised the woman at the well (see John 4)?

_____

_____

_____

_____

Repeating chorus. The following statement is repeated four times in Psalm 107: "Let them give thanks to the LORD for his unfailing love and his wonderful deeds for mankind." It was common in Hebrew poetry, especially the Psalms, to repeat a phrase to emphasize its importance. This poetic device is akin to repeating choruses of many modern-day songs. In this case, the phrase reminds the reader that he or she should be specifically thankful for God's compassion and provision in our lives.

For the group

Warm-up. Have everyone sit in a circle or around a table. Start the discussion by naming one of God's blessings in your life and why you are thankful to God for that blessing. For example, a man might say, "I consider my daughter one of God's greatest blessings in my life. I'm thankful to Him for her because she makes me understand how much God loves me as my Father in heaven." Make sure everyone has a chance to contribute a blessing and a word of thanks.

Questions. Today's questions are geared toward helping group members understand God's emotional response to our gratitude. We all know what it's like to be the recipient of someone's heartfelt gratitude—and also how we feel a bit slighted or exploited when someone we've helped forgets or refuses to say thank-you. Giving thanks also reminds us of the Source of everything we have and helps prevent us from taking for granted the everyday blessings of life.

Prayer. In today's group prayer, give everyone a chance to "count his or her blessings" by naming them specifically and giving thanks to God. Also, encourage group members to rejoice in the ways God has blessed others.

STUDY AIDS

For further information on the material in this study, consider the following sources. They are available on the Internet (www.christianbook.com, www.amazon.com, etc.) or your local Christian bookstore should be able to order any of them if it does not carry them. Most seminary libraries have them, as well as many university and public libraries.

Commentaries on Psalms

Bullock, C. Hassell. *Encountering the Book of Psalms: A Literary and Theological Introduction* (Baker Academic, 2004).
> This is a good starting point if you want to better understand the Psalms in their historical, theological, and literary contexts. Examines the different types of psalms. Provides chapter objectives and outlines, sidebars, charges, and illustrations.

Henry, Matthew. *Matthew Henry's Commentary on the Whole Bible: Volume 3: Psalms to Isaiah* (Hendrickson, 1991).
> Modern scholars have surpassed Henry in knowledge of Hebrew and the historical background of Psalms, but none surpasses him in expounding the text for the Christian reader. Henry's eighteenth-century language may be an obstacle for some readers, but it is worth getting used to. His applications are as relevant now as they were when the commentary first appeared in 1712.

Longman III, Tremper, and David E. Garland, editors, Willem A. VanGemeren, contributor. *The Expositor's Bible Commentary: Psalms* (Zondervan, 2008).
> An award-winning favorite of pastors and seminarians, this commentary is also accessible to laypeople. Draws from the insights of established biblical authorities throughout the centuries as well as the most recent evangelical scholarship. Recognizes differences of opinion among the various streams of Christendom and treats them with balance and respect.

Wilson, Gerald H. *NIV Application Commentary: Psalms,* Volume 1 (Zondervan, 2002).

The book is aptly named, as it goes beyond what many commentaries accomplish to help readers make applications to their twenty-first-century circumstances. Whereas many commentaries do a fine job of explaining the original meanings of the text, they sometimes fall short of helping readers apply ageless truths to contemporary life. If you want help understanding what the Psalms meant for ancient readers and for you, this is the book you want to get.

Historical Background Sources and Handbooks

Bible study becomes more meaningful when modern Western readers understand the times and places in which the biblical authors lived. *The IVP Bible Background Commentary: Old Testament,* by John H. Walton, Victor H. Matthews, and Mark Chavalas (InterVarsity, 2000), provides insight into the ancient Near Eastern world, its peoples, customs, and geography to help contemporary readers better understand the context in which the Old Testament Scriptures were written.

A **handbook** of biblical customs can also be useful. Some good ones are the time-proven updated classic, *Halley's Bible Handbook with the New International Version,* by Henry H. Halley (Zondervan, 2007), and the inexpensive paperback *Manners and Customs in the Bible,* by Victor H. Matthews (Hendrickson, 1991).

Concordances, Dictionaries, and Encyclopedias

A **concordance** lists words of the Bible alphabetically along with each verse in which the word appears. It lets you do your own word studies. An *exhaustive* concordance lists every word used in a given translation, while an *abridged* or *complete* concordance omits either some words, some occurrences of the word, or both.

Two of the best exhaustive concordances are *Strong's Exhaustive Concordance* and *The Strongest NIV Exhaustive Concordance. Strong's* is available based on the King James Version of the Bible and the New American Standard Bible. *Strong's* has an index by which you can find out which Greek or Hebrew word is used in a given English verse. The NIV concordance does the same thing except it also includes an index for Aramaic words in the original texts from which the NIV was translated. However, neither concordance requires knowledge of the original languages. *Strong's* is available online at www.biblestudytools.com. Both are also available in hard copy.

A **Bible dictionary** or **Bible encyclopedia** alphabetically lists articles about people, places, doctrines, important words, customs, and geography of the Bible.

Holman Illustrated Bible Dictionary, by C. Brand, C. W. Draper, and A.

England (B&H, 2003), offers more than seven hundred color photos, illustrations, and charts; sixty full-color maps; and up-to-date archeological findings, along with exhaustive definitions of people, places, things, and events—dealing with every subject in the Bible. It uses a variety of Bible translations and is the only dictionary that includes the HCSB, NIV, KJV, RSV, NRSV, REB, NASB, ESV, and TEV.

The *New Unger's Bible Dictionary, Revised and Expanded*, by Merrill F. Unger (Moody, 2006), has been a best seller for almost fifty years. Its 6,700-plus entries reflect the most current scholarship and more than 1,200,000 words are supplemented with detailed essays, colorful photography and maps, and dozens of charts and illustrations to enhance your understanding of God's Word. Based on the New American Standard Version.

The Zondervan Encyclopedia of the Bible, edited by Moisés Silva and Merrill C. Tenney (Zondervan, 2008), is excellent and exhaustive. However, its five 1,000-page volumes are a financial investment, so all but very serious students may prefer to use it at a church, public, college, or seminary library.

Unlike a Bible dictionary in the above sense, *Vine's Complete Expository Dictionary of Old and New Testament Words,* by W. E. Vine, Merrill F. Unger, and William White Jr. (Thomas Nelson, 1996), alphabetically lists major words used in the King James Version and defines each Old Testament Hebrew or New Testament Greek word the KJV translates with that English word. *Vine's* lists verse references where that Hebrew or Greek word appears so that you can do your own cross-references and word studies without knowing the original languages.

The Brown-Driver-Briggs Hebrew and English Lexicon by Francis Brown, C. Briggs, and S. R. Driver (Hendrickson, 1996), is probably the most respected and comprehensive Bible lexicon for Old Testament studies. *BDB* gives not only dictionary definitions for each word but relates each word to its Old Testament usage and categorizes its nuances of meaning.

Bible Atlases and Map Books

A **Bible atlas** can be a great aid to understanding what is going on in a book of the Bible and how geography affected events. Here are a few good choices:

The Hammond Atlas of Bible Lands (Langenscheidt, 2007) packs a ton of resources into just sixty-four pages. Maps, of course, but also photographs, illustrations, and a comprehensive timeline. Includes an introduction to the unique geography of the Holy Land, including terrain, trade routes, vegetation, and climate information.

The New Moody Atlas of the Bible, by Barry J. Beitzel (Moody, 2009), is scholarly, very evangelical, and full of theological text, indexes, and references. Beitzel shows vividly how God prepared the land of Israel perfectly for the acts of salvation He was going to accomplish in it.

Then and Now Bible Maps Insert (Rose, 2008) is a nifty paperback that is sized just right to fit inside your Bible cover. Only forty-four pages long, it features clear plastic overlays of modern-day cities and countries so you can see what nation or city now occupies the Bible setting you are reading about. Every major city of the Bible is included.

For Small-Group Leaders

Discipleship Journal's Best Small-Group Ideas, Volumes 1 and 2 (NavPress, 2005).
Each volume is packed with 101 of the best hands-on tips and group-building principles from *Discipleship Journal's* "Small Group Letter" and "DJ Plus" as well as articles from the magazine. They will help you inject new passion into the life of your small group.

Donahue, Bill. *Leading Life-Changing Small Groups* (Zondervan, 2002).
This comprehensive resource is packed with information, practical tips, and insights that will teach you about small-group philosophy and structure, discipleship, conducting meetings, and more.

McBride, Neal F. *How to Build a Small-Groups Ministry* (NavPress, 1994).
How to Build a Small-Groups Ministry is a time-proven, hands-on workbook for pastors and lay leaders that includes everything you need to know to develop a plan that fits your unique church. Through basic principles, case studies, and worksheets, McBride leads you through twelve logical steps for organizing and administering a small-groups ministry.

McBride, Neal F. *How to Lead Small Groups* (NavPress, 1990).
This book covers leadership skills for all kinds of small groups: Bible study, fellowship, task, and support groups. Filled with step-by-step guidance and practical exercises to help you grasp the critical aspects of small-group leadership and dynamics.

Miller, Tara, and Jenn Peppers. *Finding the Flow: A Guide for Leading Small Groups and Gatherings* (IVP Connect, 2008).
Finding the Flow offers a fresh take on leading small groups by seeking to develop the leader's small-group facilitation skills.

Bible Study Methods

Discipleship Journal's Best Bible Study Methods (NavPress, 2002).
This is a collection of thirty-two creative ways to explore Scripture that will help you enjoy studying God's Word more.

Hendricks, Howard, and William Hendricks. *Living by the Book: The Art and Science of Reading the Bible* (Moody, 2007).
Living by the Book offers a practical three-step process that will help you master simple yet effective inductive methods of observation,

interpretation, and application that will make all the difference in your time with God's Word. A workbook by the same title is also available to go along with the book.

The Navigator Bible Studies Handbook (NavPress, 1994).
This resource teaches the underlying principles for doing good inductive Bible study, including instructions on doing queston-and-answer studies, verse-analysis studies, chapter-analysis studies, and topical studies.

Warren, Rick. *Rick Warren's Bible Study Methods: Twelve Ways You Can Unlock God's Word* (HarperCollins, 2006).
Rick Warren offers simple, step-by-step instructions, guiding you through twelve different approaches to studying the Bible for yourself with the goal of becoming more like Jesus.

BULK PRICING
Is Available

Order enough for everyone in your group!

SUPPORT THE MINISTRY OF THE NAVIGATORS

The Navigators' calling is to advance the Gospel of Jesus and His Kingdom into the nations through spiritual generations of laborers living and discipling among the lost.

Navigators have invested their lives in people for more than 75 years, coming alongside them life-on-life to help them passionately know Christ and to make Him known.

The U.S. Navigators' ministry touches lives in varied settings, including college campuses, military bases, downtown offices, and urban neighborhoods, prisons, and youth camps.

Dedicated to helping people navigate spiritually, The Navigators aim to make a permanent difference in the lives of people around the world. The Navigators help their communities of friends to follow Christ passionately and equip them effectively to go out and do the same.

To learn more about donating to The Navigators' ministry, go to **www.navigators.org/us/support** or call toll-free at **1-866-568-7827**.